# Fresh Spring

# Fresh Spring

Gregory Chigozie Nnaji

authorHOUSE

*AuthorHouse™*
*1663 Liberty Drive*
*Bloomington, IN 47403*
*www.authorhouse.com*
*Phone: 833-262-8899*

*Published by AuthorHouse 10/27/2023*

*ISBN: 978-1-4634-3662-9 (sc)*
*ISBN: 978-1-4634-3661-2 (hc)*
*ISBN: 978-1-4634-3660-5 (e)*

*Library of Congress Control Number: 2011912762*

*Print information available on the last page.*

*This book is printed on acid-free paper.*

# CONTENTS

# *Abbreviations*

All Scriptural quotations in this book are taken from the New International Version unless otherwise stated.

The following abbreviations are used in this book to identify English translations of the Bible:

KJV: King James Version
NKJV: New King James Version
NIV: New International Version

# Dedication

To my beloved family for their unflinching support.

# Foreword

Gregory Nnaji revives the spirit of the early twentieth century Christian writers. Unlike the vast majority of authors today that focus on how-tos and building a better me, Gregory places his emphasis on the supremacy of Christ and His work within the believer. His books are birthed out of personal prayer, struggle, and the inspiration of the Holy Spirit. Gregory's latest work is no exception.

Fresh Spring is, as the title implies, a fresh perspective on the power of God working within the believer. Ranging from subjects such as the near insanity of rebellion against God, to the blessedness of unity, Fresh Spring takes the reader on a spiritual journey that challenges the heart and satiates the soul. The focus is on the believer who wants more, who is searching for depth in his or her Christian experience. The reader will especially find the personal stories of struggle and victory, born out of Gregory's recent past, to bring life to the chapters as well as offer practical application to the topics studied. Thanks to the transparent words of Fresh Spring, you may very well feel that you have known Gregory for a long time!

I have been blessed to be Gregory's pastor and have witnessed firsthand his deep commitment to Christ and loving expression of the Christian faith. He and his family have made great sacrifices to serve God wholeheartedly. I trust that you will find his spiritual memoirs of Fresh Spring as a catalyst for a deeper, fresher relationship with Christ.

For Christ's Glory,

Rev. Michael Darretta
Pastor and Author

# Preface

My foremost gratitude goes to God, who inspired the writing of this book and guided its production. I owe Him my life and aspirations.

I also wish to express my immense thanks to Pastor Mike Darretta, who graciously took the pains of proofreading the manuscript and writing its foreword. To me, that was a great honor.

Finally, I am indebted to my beloved wife, Ifeoma, and children for their patience, understanding, and support while I toiled to put the book together. They have been co-laborers with me in God's vineyard, and I feel thoroughly blessed by them.

May God bless you all and others, not mentioned herein, who made any contributions toward the production of the book.

Fresh Spring is a stream of inspired messages meant to provide nourishment and inspiration to keep believers shining and vibrant in the Lord. It also aims at attracting and challenging unbelievers to find life that is life indeed in Jesus Christ.

We live in an era of gross dilution of the word of God for selfish gains with the result that many grope in the dark in their Christian lives. Consequently, God continues to lament: "my people are destroyed from lack of knowledge . . ." (Hos. 4: 6). In this book, however, I have made a spirited effort to present the truth of the word of God so clearly that everyone will understand and no one will be in doubt about what God expects of him. It is my earnest prayer that as one goes through the book, he will know the truth and the truth will set him free (Jn. 8:32).

Gregory Chigozie Nnaji

# Chapter One

## Mad Fellows of a Sort

The simplest definition of a mad fellow is someone out of his senses—someone who is insane. The most common manifestations of madness are consistently foolish or irrational behavior and incoherent speech.

Jesus gave an instructive account of "insanity" of a sort in Luke 15:11-24. Hear the story:

> [11]Jesus continued: "There was a man who had two sons. [12]The younger one said to his father, 'Father, give me my share of the estate.' So he divided his property between them.
>
> [13]"Not long after that, the younger son got together all he had, set off for a distant country and there squandered his wealth in wild living.
>
> [14]After he had spent everything, there was a severe famine in that whole country, and he began to be in need.
>
> [15]So he went and hired himself out to a citizen of that country, who sent him to his fields to feed pigs.

[16]He longed to fill his stomach with the pods that the pigs were eating, but no one gave him anything.

[17]"When he came to his senses, he said, 'How many of my father's hired men have food to spare, and here I am starving to death!

[18]I will set out and go back to my father and say to him: Father, I have sinned against heaven and against you.

[19]I am no longer worthy to be called your son; make me like one of your hired men.'

[20]So he got up and went to his father. "But while he was still a long way off, his father saw him and was filled with compassion for him; he ran to his son, threw his arms around him and kissed him.

[21]"The son said to him, 'Father, I have sinned against heaven and against you. I am no longer worthy to be called your son.'

[22]"But the father said to his servants, 'Quick! Bring the best robe and put it on him. Put a ring on his finger and sandals on his feet.

[23]Bring the fattened calf and kill it. Let's have a feast and celebrate.

[24]For this son of mine was dead and is alive again; he was lost and is found.' So they began to celebrate.

From the story, a few days after the younger son received his own share of his father's possessions, he packed all his belongings and left for a far country. Why did he choose a far country? He wanted a place where his father would not see him to caution or advise him. He wanted freedom from all forms of control. In the distant country, he found such freedom and the consequence was wild living. When a young man who has some wealth is said to live wild, what picture do we see? We see a picture of a young man who lives in luxury; one who drives big and expensive cars, moves with hordes of women and friends, indulges in excessive drinking, attends wild parties, lives in hotels and embarks on lavish spending. The young man in the story obviously lived like that. He did not make any investments with his money but wasted it. He did not remember tomorrow.

Of course, we know that when he was "on," he was the "happening guy" in town—the toast of society. He was the envy of many a young man. Fans trooped after him, and many people wanted to be his friend. He was indeed the center of attraction. He was "the lord."

For a guy in that state, he was high in spirit—no time to think, no time to plan, no moments of silence. It was all action, all fun—enjoyment galore! He had no time to remember that his money could someday run out. He simply felt okay with himself. He had no time to notice that his money was running out until it was gone.

His money ran out about the time there was great famine in the country. Because he had made neither savings nor investments, he soon began to starve. So he hired himself to a local farmer who sent him into his pig farm to feed pigs. There, he felt so hungry that he desired to feed on the pods with which he fed the pigs, "but no one gave him anything." Pity! From grace to grass.

One day, however, something startling happened. Verses 17-18 of the text says, "he came to his senses . . . ."

What does this imply? It implies that until now, he was out of his senses. What does it mean to be out of one's senses? It means to be crazy. It means to be mad. Instructively, this is "madness" of a sort—an unusual type describing a child's rebellion from godly parental control. That means that right from the time he conceived the idea of leaving home for a distant country with his possessions for lavish lifestyle, he was out of his senses. All the while he was in the country living in exquisite comfort and luxury and hailed by young men and ladies, he was "mad." All the time he was the toast of all, he was "crazy." Even when he exhausted his wealth and hired himself out to a pig farmer to feed pigs, he was out of his senses. He remained out of his senses until that day and that very hour when he came to his senses. He then regained his sanity.

When he came to his senses, he realized he was in the wrong place and doing the wrong things. He remembered his roots. He remembered his father and said, "How many of my father's hired men have food to spare, and here I am starving to death! I will set out and go to my father . . ." (vs. 17-18). He realized his folly and decided to retrace his steps. He decided to go back to his father.

From the story, we see that anybody who lives unto himself is out of his senses. Anyone who lives freely and without regard to God's instructions is in a distant country far away from God. Such a person is out of his senses. So is anyone who merely lives for pleasure and has no plan for tomorrow (tomorrow in this case meaning life hereafter). Anyone who indulges in wild living is out of his senses. In fact, to put it straight, every sinner (i.e., anyone who lives in sin) is out of his senses. Note the word "anyone" or "anybody." That means whosoever without exceptions. Hence, irrespective of your political, economic, social, and religious status, intellectual attainment, age, sex, or color, you are not in your senses if you are living wild—without recourse to God, your Maker and Owner.

You are living in a far country, away from your Father, God. You need to come to your senses. You need to retrace your steps and return to God. You need to take a cue from the young man in our story. In your wild life, you have covered yourself with sin just like a mad fellow covers himself with filth. Sin is filth and stinks. You need to remove your filthy garment of sin.

**Irrespective of your political, economic, social, and religious status, intellectual attainment, age, sex, or color, you are not in your senses if you are living wild—without recourse to God, your Maker and Owner.**

Let us look again at what the young man did when he came to his senses as a guide. He said, "I will set out and go to my father and say to him: 'Father, I have sinned against heaven and against you. I am no longer worthy to be called your son; make me like one of your hired men'" (vs. 17-19). A little analysis of the above statement will help us. When he realized himself, he saw himself for who he was—a sinner. He saw his filthiness and unworthiness. Hence, he acknowledged that he had sinned against heaven and against his father. He was ready and willing to accept the privilege of being regarded as his father's hired servant. He knew he had lost his position and right of inheritance in the family. Having acknowledged his true status, he made a decision: "I will set out and go to my father and say to him: 'Father, I have sinned against heaven and against you . . . .'" He decided to own up his sin and ask for forgiveness. That is instructive. He decided not to continue his wayward life. He decided to head home. That is a sign of sanity. The next verse (verse 20) then says, "So he got up and went to his father." The young man did not stop at the point of decision, but followed it up with action. That is noteworthy. If he had remained in that country, there would have been no evidence that he had become sane, and he would not have had the privilege of receiving his father's pardon. He would have perished in that far country bearing his sin and guilt. He would not have noticed that his father eagerly anticipated his return and was ready to receive him back into the family not as a servant, but as a son. The young man actually arose and went to his father.

The account shows that while he was still a long way off, his father saw him and was filled with compassion for him and ran to his son and embraced him and kissed him. Amazing, isn't it? The young man then confessed his sin as he had earlier decided. Let us consider the implications of his father's actions:

1.  He saw his son while he was still a long way off. That is a sign that he had been anticipating his son's return. He had been looking forward to seeing him come back.
2.  He was filled with compassion, implying mercy and readiness to receive him.
3.  He ran to meet his son, implying eagerness to receive him.
4.  He embraced and kissed him, which shows reception and love. The young man was quite welcome. Notice, however, that despite his father's warm welcome, the young man went ahead and confessed his sin. He did not presume that all was well because of the way he was received. This again is instructive.

The father then quickly ordered his servants to bring the best robe and put it on him, put a ring on his finger and sandals on his feet. He ordered also that a fattened calf be brought and killed, and a feast be promptly organized because his son who was dead was alive again and who was lost was found. So a big feast ensued.

The young man's father more than granted his son's request. He forgave his sin and accepted him back, not as a servant but as a son. He said: "For this son of mine was dead and is alive again; he was lost but is found" (verse 24). He referred to him as a son, not a servant. He ordered that his filthy garment of sin be removed and replaced with "the best robe," plus a ring and sandals to match. This child was fully reabsorbed into his father's family, with the ring signifying the reunion.

Notice that the son retained the filthy garment of sin until he got to his father. Only his father, against whom he had sinned, had the authority to order its removal after forgiving him. If the father did not forgive him, he would have retained the garment for life. If the son had stopped at the point of decision to go to his father and did not act, he would have retained the garment for as long as he remained there. If the son had stopped anywhere on the way to his father's house, he would have retained that filthy garment. He had to meet his father, confess his sin to his father, and receive his father's forgiveness to have that garment removed.

Now let us consider the cue you need from the young man's story. I have already noted that as long as you are living in sin, you are out of your senses—insane. You need to come to yourself and return to your Father, God. Here is an outline of the steps the young man took, which you need to take also:

1.  He acknowledged his sin and was sorry about it;
2.  He decided to go back to his father;
3.  He followed his decision up by actually arising and going to his father;
4.  He confessed his sin to his father and asked for forgiveness.

You need to follow these steps and return to God, your heavenly Father. Do not skip any of them.

There is good news for you. The good news is that, like in the young man's case, your heavenly Father is eagerly awaiting your return. See what He has in store for you:

— He will extend His compassion to you;

— He will warmly embrace you and welcome you;

— He will forgive your sins;

— He will remove your filthy garment of sin and clothe you with the garment of righteousness;

— He will put a ring in your finger as a sign of your union with Him;

— He will throw a party in heaven to celebrate your return; and,

— He will make you His son.

This is amazing. Why wait any longer? Why not embrace the wonderful opportunity and privilege now? God is saying to you, "behold now is the accepted time; behold, now is the day of salvation" (11 Cor. 6:2). Tomorrow may be too late. Return now.

# Chapter Two

## Loyalty to the Devil: Gains and Losses

In this discussion, I will analyze the pros and cons of being loyal to the devil. I shall be doing this by looking at a few biblical accounts. In Matthew 4: 1-11, we read about the temptation of Jesus by the devil. Verses 8-10 say:

> [8]Again, the devil took him to a very high mountain and showed him all the kingdoms of the world and their splendor.
> [9]'All this I will give you,' he said, 'if you will bow down and worship me.'
> [10]Jesus said to him, "Away from me, Satan! For it is written: 'Worship the Lord your God, and serve him only."

Here, the devil offers Jesus all the kingdoms of the world if he should bow down and worship him, but Jesus declines the offer and chooses to worship only God. He chooses to obey the Scripture rather than the devil.

Now let us look at the gains and losses that would have accrued to Jesus if He had bowed and worshipped the devil. He would have gained the following:

1. The kingdoms of the world, but for a short while—the rest of His life on earth, maybe.
2. Spared the sorrow and shame of the cross.

The losses, on the other hand, would have been as follows:

1. Loss of His relationship with His Father, God.
2. Loss of the eternal glory and joy that awaited Him (Lk. 24: 26; Heb. 12: 2).
3. Loss of the position reserved for Him after the cross: highest position and name above all names—authority over the universe.
4. Loss of soul (Matthew 16: 26).

Jesus began His ministry at the age of thirty, and that was when the devil tempted Him. He was destined to live for only thirty three years; hence, He had only three years left. Had He bowed down and worshipped the devil, He would have gained all the kingdoms of the world and the glory thereof for only three years at the most. Note that the devil did not promise Him a longer life, as he had no power to do so. Jesus would have therefore gained rulership over the world for three years only and He would have lost everlasting rulership over heaven, earth, and beneath the earth reserved for Him by God. And what is three years compared to eternity? The devil remains a deceiver and will usually offer what looks like an attractive pleasure while blinding one to the fleeting nature of the offering. The Scripture describes it as the "fleeting pleasures of sin" (Heb. 11: 26)—the pleasures of sin that last for a short while. He would then make Him throw away the eternal glory that God kept in store for Him. Whatever pleasure the devil offers is temporary. It can only last for a little while—a lifetime, at the most. And what is a lifetime compared to eternity?

In the case of Jesus, it would have lasted just for three years. But what God gives endures forever. Do not be deceived. Look well before you accept the devil's short-cut pleasure. His offering is usually a whitewashed tomb that looks attractive on the surface but contains rot on the inside. The end of every gift of the devil is destruction. He will usually coat sin with sweetness to conceal its sting. Beware! Had He consented to the devil, Jesus would have had eternal losses—His relationship with His Father; glory; position; and soul.

> **Whatever pleasure the devil offers is temporary. It can only last for a little while—a lifetime, at the most. And what is a lifetime compared to eternity?**

At another time, just after Peter had identified Jesus as the Messiah (Christ) by revelation, Jesus began to explain to His disciples that He must go to Jerusalem and suffer many things at the hands of the elders, chief priests, and teachers of the law, and that He must be killed and on the third day be raised to life (Matthew 16: 13-27). He began to tell them about the cross. Satan entered Peter and sought through him to dissuade Jesus from accepting the cross. Peter took Him aside and began to rebuke Him, saying, "Never Lord! This shall never happen to you!" Peter wanted Jesus to come to His senses so to speak: "You, the Messiah, suffering? Never! Don't say this! Don't even think about it!" He wanted Him to realize the contradiction in being a Messiah and talking about suffering. This is very like what the devil still says today, "If you are a child of God, why do you suffer? A child of God should never suffer." People said the same thing to Jesus during His crucifixion, "Save yourself!

Come down from the cross, if you are the son of God!" (Matthew 27:39-40). They did not realize that it was appointed by God for Jesus to suffer these things before entering His glory (Luke 24:26). It is same for all of God's children. Every one of us must first bear his own cross before entering His glory.

Jesus realized it was the devil speaking through Peter. He realized where He was going—to paint the picture of a glamorous and all-powerful Messiah who sits on a throne and wields power and authority as against the suffering Messiah, who gave His life to redeem mankind. Immediately, He turned to Peter and retorted, "Get behind me, Satan! You are a stumbling block to me; you do not have in mind the things of God, but the things of men" (Matthew 16:23). He knew that Satan wanted to distract Him and make Him think of the Messiah from the human point of view. He rejected Satan and his odious insinuation. Once again, He proved consistent in His choices, insisting on always obeying God.

He then went ahead and clearly stated the conditions for following Him:

> If anyone would come after me, he must deny himself and take up his cross and follow me. For whoever wants to save his life will lose it, but whoever loses his life for me will find it. What good will it be for a man if he gains the whole world, yet forfeits his soul? Or what can a man give in exchange for his soul? (Matthew 16: 24-26).

Only those who understand the conditions and adopt them follow Him—follow Him through the way of the cross and ultimately into His glory.

Moses was another man who looked beyond the present and chose a later glory with God. The Scripture says that by faith Moses, when he had grown up, refused to be known as the son of Pharaoh's daughter. He chose to be mistreated along with the people of God rather than to enjoy the pleasures of sin for a short time. He regarded disgrace for the sake of Christ as of greater value than the treasures of Egypt, because he was looking ahead to his reward from God (Heb. 11: 24-26). He had the opportunity to enjoy a lifetime of royalty in Pharaoh's house, having been raised son of Pharaoh's daughter. But he knew he belonged to the suffering people of Israel. He chose to identify with his suffering people because he knew that the pleasures of Egypt were transient. He also knew that they were the people of God. A choice to remain in the house of Pharaoh would have earned him enmity with God. He chose to obey God. He eventually became the most revered leader of Israel ever. The best he would have gained from Pharaoh's house would have been a royal lifestyle for life. He would never have become the king, since Pharaoh had his own son. He would have lost the opportunity to be the greatest leader of Israel and would have lost his soul in hell eventually.

Joseph is yet another example. In the house of Potiphar, he was placed in charge of his master's household and business. He was totally in charge. Then the devil came and tempted him through Potiphar's wife. She wanted him to sleep with her. Joseph said to her, "How then could I do such a wicked thing and sin against God?" (Gen. 39:9). Though she spoke to him day after day, Joseph refused to sleep with her or even to be with her. Amazing! See what attraction obeying her held for Joseph:

13

1. Retention of his position and authority over his master's household and business. He would have retained his CEO position, possibly for a lifetime.
2. He would have been spared the pain and agony of imprisonment.

But he would have lost the following:

1. His relationship and favor with God.
2. The position of prime minister of Egypt and the worldwide fame that came with it.
3. He would have lost his soul in hell.

Let us, on the contrary, take examples of people who gave in to the devil. In Matthew 4:2-4, we read that after Jesus had fasted for forty days and forty nights he was hungry. The devil came to him and said, "If you are the son of God, command these stones to become bread." But Jesus answered him saying, "It is written, 'Man does not live on bread alone, but on every word that comes from the mouth of God.'" Thus, Jesus defeated the devil. But there was another man in the Scripture who sold his birthright for food. His name was Esau. The account, found in Genesis 25: 29-34, reads:

> <sup>29</sup>Once when Jacob was cooking some stew, Esau came in from the open country, famished.
> <sup>30</sup>He said to Jacob, "Quick, let me have some of that red stew! I'm famished!" (That is why he was also called Edom.)
> <sup>31</sup>Jacob replied, "First sell me your birthright."
> <sup>32</sup>"Look, I am about to die," Esau said. "What good is the birthright to me?"

<sup>33</sup>But Jacob said, "Swear to me first." So he swore an oath to him, selling his birthright to Jacob.

<sup>34</sup>Then Jacob gave Esau some bread and some lentil stew. He ate and drank, and then got up and left.

So Esau despised his birthright.

What did Esau gain by giving in to the temptation? Momentary satisfaction from the food he ate. What did he lose? His inheritance, favor with God, and covenant relationship with God. He was rejected by God. The devil will usually trivialize the invaluable benefit God has for us in order to deceive us. Thus, Esau despised his birthright, saying, "What good is the birthright to me?" Yet, later, he sought it with tears but did not get it (Heb. 12: 16, 17). He lost it forever, for no one can have his cake and eat it. How painful!

> **The devil will usually trivialize the invaluable benefit God has for us in order to deceive us.**

Another biblical example of one who chose to obey the devil is Adam and Eve. God had given the fruits of all the trees in the Garden of Eden as food for Adam and Eve but asked them not to eat or touch the fruits of one tree in the middle of the garden or they would die. The serpent said to Eve, "You will not surely die. For God knows that when you eat of it, your eyes will be opened, and you will be like God, knowing good and evil" (Gen. 3: 4-5). He portrayed God as a deceiver. The woman believed him, took some of the fruits of the tree and ate, and gave some to her husband, Adam, and he ate also. The serpent made her pay attention to the tree to notice how attractive the fruits were. She got captivated and she ate it and she went further to entice her husband into eating it too. What did they gain? Momentary satisfaction from the fruit. What did they lose? Fellowship with God and the beautiful garden. That fall brought about the downfall of mankind. It enthroned sin and the consequences of sin—death, diseases, and all kinds of suffering (Gen. 3: 1-24; Rom. 5: 12; Rom. 6: 23).

The devil continues to deceive people by magnifying the momentary satisfaction from sin while blinding them to the eternal rewards of obedience to God. His ploy is to overwhelm people with passion for sinful pleasures. Once he enthrones passion, reason is cast overboard until the sin is committed. Once the sin is committed and the momentary pleasure dissipates, the full consequence follows. The common areas of his deception include sex, money, fame, and power. Sexual immorality, for instance, has become the order of the day in our world today. Sex appeal has become so pervasive. You see it on television, newspapers, and the Internet. Virtually all TV movies, all newspaper, radio, and Internet adverts, product flyers, billboards, secular novels, etc. have sex appeal. It looks like no product can sell without sex appeal. In our time, to look good means to look "sexy." In fact, life has been defined to be all about sex. Children imbibe this definition from TV movies and adverts and from the dressings of adults all around them. Passion for it is right on the throne in our society today. Promiscuity has become normal and no more an absurdity. Characteristically, the devil has concealed all the inherent dangers of promiscuity—unwanted pregnancy, disease, and death. No one remembers its spiritual consequences either—the facts that it is sinful and attracts the wages of sin, which is death. Young people freely adopt promiscuous lifestyles with its destructive consequences. In the name of freedom, all kinds of sexual pervasion have become prevalent. Things that were unthinkable in the past have become normal today. Horrible!

> **The devil continues to deceive people by magnifying the momentary satisfaction from sin while blinding them to the eternal rewards of obedience to God.**

There is, of course, no gain-saying that people do anything for money, fame, and power. The craving for these things has stifled every sense of reason and conscience such that people do incalculable things to get them. These are all orchestrated by the devil and are ravaging the world.

It is heartening to know, however, that despite the prevalence of these delusions, God still has a remnant who are still careful to follow and obey Him—who still turn down the gold-coated sinful offerings of the devil. Just like the Scripture testifies of some men of faith in Hebrews 11:35 who were tortured and who refused to be released so that they might gain a better resurrection, there are still Christians in our day who insist on obeying God rather than the devil and who pay great prices for that. So many of them are found in Islamic and communist countries where the Christian faith is illegal. A few examples will make the point clear. Let us see the story of Sabina Wurmbrand. She and her husband, Richard, were Christian converts in 1930s and 1940s in Romania and founded an underground church in the country. She was arrested for secret Christian activities that also included smuggling Jewish children out of the ghettos.

At a point, the Romanian Communist Party sponsored a "religious conference" and ministers were required not only to attend but also to profess loyalty to Communism. Sabina insisted that her husband should stand up for Christ, even if that would leave her a widow. She told Richard, "I don't wish to have a coward for a husband." In the presence of four thousand spectators and as the whole nation listened on the radio, Richard Wurmbrand professed allegiance only to Jesus Christ.

As a result, he was imprisoned, placed in solitary confinement, and tortured for years.

Sabina herself spent much time both in prison and under house arrest. She told the shocking stories of how Christian women were made to work for hours at slave labor, scooping out a canal by hand; and how though bone-tired, the women were kept awake by empty stomach at night. She told how the captors gathered children and beat them up in the camp just to torment their parents. She recalled how she wondered about her nine-year-old son, Mihai, now a homeless orphan. The wardens promised to let the women see their children only if they kept laboring, and that hope kept them alive and working even when all heart and strength were gone. Eventually, the day came when Sabina would meet with Mihai. She had only a few minutes, and her heart was too full for speech. The little boy was pale and thin. As the boy was led away, she managed to say, "Mihai, love Jesus with all your heart!"

Finally, the Wurmbrand family pulled through those dark days as strong Christians (Wurmbrand 1998; Jeremiah 2009).

Here again is another gruesome story of four Christian young men in North Korea:

> The report from The Voice of the Martyrs tells of four young men who chose pseudonyms—Pencil, Eraser, Pen, and Paper Clip—while training for a Christian mission expedition into North Korea.
>
> They were trained by "Andrew," a Christian worker in China, for the work that would face them after crossing the Tumen River into North Korea.
>
> While the three were studious in their work the VOM report said, the young man who chose

the name "Pencil" seemed to pay little attention, but all four were dispatched into the kingdom of Kim Jong-il a short time later.

Reports from within North Korea several months later came to VOM that three—Eraser, Pen, and Paper Clip—had been arrested by North Korean police and beaten, thrown into vehicles, and taken away. Reports came back the three were in a concentration camp, and Pencil, who had watched the arrests, never saw them again.

Pencil, who feared a similar arrest, lived as a beggar to avoid detection, and then returned to Andrew in China.

With tears in his eyes, "Pencil" told Andrew the fate of his three friends. He shared how they had been bold witnesses for Christ, and how he had hid in fear as his best friends were taken away, the report, written by P. Todd Nettleton, said.

"What do you want to do with the rest of your life?" Andrew asked, and Pencil told him, "I want to learn how to be brave like my friends, and unafraid to share Jesus."

The boy whose mind always seemed to wander was now a young man completely committed to Christ, the VOM report said. When Pencil was ready to return to North Korea, he looked into the eyes of his friend and mentor and said, "I need nothing more."

He immediately connected with a Christian couple inside North Korea, and together they worked on their ministry. For five months, they planted seeds of faith and prayed.

"One day the three of them were sharing with a small group of beggars and gave them some tracts and a Bible. One of the young beggars went home and proudly showed the Bible to his mother," VOM's report said.

The mother promptly grabbed it and marched into a police station, where commanders dispatched officers to arrest the couple and Pencil.

His following interrogation quickly turned to torture as officers demanded to know the source of the Bible, and that Pencil recant.

Instead, he told them of his friends and their fearless witness.

"There was a time when I couldn't be like them," he said. "I was too afraid. But now I can be since Jesus is with me."

Beatings and torture, including pulling out his fingernails, followed.

"If you kill me, someday you will become a Christian," Pencil told the officers.

Eventually, the officers gave up, ordering him to a labor camp but with instructions that he not be fed. For two months, Pencil told the other prisoners and the camp guards, "Jesus is the reason I am able to go on."

Because of his endurance and how he shared the love of Jesus, many in the camp turned to Christ, the VOM report said. After two months in the camp, Pencil died. He never saw his twentieth birthday. His body was removed from the camp, but the fruit of his short ministry there lived on.

(WorldNetDaily, "Teen's testimony of faith unstopped by death," posted by Anonymous, October 26, 2006, accessed February 12, 2011, http://www.wndcom/?pageId=38540).

I will not fail to talk about the pathetic and yet inspiring story I read from a recent publication of the *The Voice of the Martyrs* about a young boy, Pelagius. Here is the account:

Pelagius was a young boy in Cordoba, Spain, who was martyred by the Muslim emir. Tenth century Cordoba was the most powerful of the Muslim caliphates in the world, boasting the largest mosque outside of Mecca. A number of Christians died for their faith in Cordoba, and Pelagius was the youngest.

Pelagius was left with the Moors (or Muslims) by his uncle at age ten. He was supposed to be ransomed, but the promised ransom never came. So Pelagius lived for three years in the court of Emir Abd al-Rahman III. Throughout his captivity, Pelagius prayed and held to his Christian faith.

When Pelagius was thirteen, the emir summoned Pelagius into his presence. He was impressed by the boy's potential and even promised to liberate him and give him many favors. The emir would give Pelagius money, fine clothes, horses to ride, and increasing honors if he would do one thing: renounce his Christian faith and accept Mohammed as his prophet.

Instead, Pelagius confessed his Christian faith and told the emir he was ready to die for it. "I am a Christian, and will remain a Christian, and obey only Christ's commands all the days of my life," Pelagius said.

The emir was filled with rage and commanded the guards to suspend Pelagius by iron tongs and haul him up and down until he renounced Christ. After suffering excruciating torture for more than six hours, Pelagius still refused to recant, saying, "O Lord, deliver me out of the hands of my enemies." The emir ordered that he be cut into pieces, and his body parts were thrown into the river.

The Christians in Cordoba retrieved his torn limbs and buried them. The story of Pelagius' bravery captured the hearts of many Spanish Christians, and many churches in Spain are named for him. ( Voice of Martyrs Blog; "Pelagius-AD 925," blog entry by Karen, October 4, 2010)

Those brethren chose to lose their lives for the sake of Jesus and the gospel. Jesus says such people will find their lives (Matt. 10:39), for we know that to be absent from the body is to be present with God (2 Cor. 5:8). And great is their reward in heaven.

Those are testimonies of severe physical persecution. Besides such, we are daily faced with situations that demand that we make choices of who to obey—God or devil. I recall one of my experiences. I am gifted with abundant soccer talent, and I planned to play professional soccer. To my surprise, all my efforts to travel abroad to pursue a soccer career when I was young and fit failed. In frustration, I kept asking God why he would not let me make use of the talent He gave me. Not playing professional soccer became my greatest regret. One day, as I continued to inquire of the Lord on the matter, He said to me, "Son, if I had allowed you play soccer, you would have made money and fame but you would have lost your faith." Immediately, I surrendered to the sovereign will of God, and my frustration vanished. I asked myself, What will it profit you to gain the whole world and lose your soul? It is not that playing professional soccer is wrong or sinful and will necessarily take someone to hell. No! It is that God is all knowing and, in my particular case, He knew that the money and fame that would come with it would sweep me away from faith as I was then a very young believer. I understood that, given my age in faith, I would be unable to manage the money and fame that professional soccer would give me and still keep my faith. Therefore, He kept me from going into the profession because He values the salvation of my soul more than any material blessings I could wish for.

Suppose I insisted on having my way, and God decided to let me. I would have probably gained millions of dollars and world-wide fame, but I would have lost my salvation and precious soul. As Jesus asks, "What can a man give in exchange for his soul?" (Matthew 16: 26). No man in his right senses will exchange his soul for ephemeral things, but the devil blinds people to this eternal truth. He highlights the "gains"—the glamour and fanfare. This is how he deceived the prodigal son in Luke 15: 11-32. He showed him the world and the "glory" thereof. He got attracted and went for it. He asked for his own share of inheritance from his father, received it, and off he went to explore and enjoy life in a far country. As the Scripture describes it, he "squandered his wealth in wild living" (v. 13). He spent everything. Thereafter, he faced the reality of his wasteful living. He began to be in need. He became hungry and hired himself to a farmer who sent him into his fields to feed pigs. And, "he longed to fill his stomach with the pods that the pigs were eating, but no one gave him anything" (v. 16). No one gave him anything—not even the food the pigs ate. He was dying of hunger. He faced the stack reality of wasteful life—the reality the devil closed his eyes and understanding to. The devil had deluded him into believing that life would remain rosy for him for life. He had hidden the thorns of life from him and shown him only the roses. Save for the intervention of the Holy Spirit, who brought him to his senses through what he suffered, his soul would have ended up in hell. He was blinded to the ugly consequences of wasteful living.

Unfortunately, many are still so blinded to the ugly consequences of sinful living, even now. They are still swimming in the ocean of sinful pleasures, thinking that is all about life. They do not understand that they are cruising and drifting into destruction—eternal destruction at that. As the Scripture says, "the wages of sin is death . . ." (Rom. 6:23). The devil who deceives people has a three-fold ministry: to steal, kill, and destroy (John 10: 10), but people do not realize it. He brainwashes them by showing them pictures that appeal to their senses. They get caught up and enjoy sensuality to their doom. Oh, that men would be alert to the wiles of the devil; that men would embrace wisdom; that men would know that all that glitters is not gold. Oh, that men would realize that behind the apparent glamorous appearances of sinful pleasures is a pang of death.

Note that the devil, most times, does not force people to obey him. He may besiege you with alluring offers, but still lets you make the choice. You are still responsible for your choices. May we be wise and farsighted. May we look before we leap. May we pause and ponder. May we consider the consequences of our choices before we make them. May we cease to act on the spur of the moment, which the devil masterminds. May we cease to base our choices just on the now gain. May we think of the afterwards. May we take a cue from men in the Bible who made wise choices, who turned down the deceptive pleasures of sin that the devil offered, and who chose to obey God though it appeared unattractive to do so—men like Jesus, Moses, and Joseph, among others. Let us choose to obey God even if it entails suffering, for, at the end, we will earn an unimaginable glory that will endure forever.

> **Let us choose to obey God even if it entails suffering, for, at the end, we will earn an unimaginable glory that will endure forever.**

# Chapter Three

# When God's Mercy Comes to an End

The Scripture variously depicts God as merciful and gracious, slow to anger, and abounding in mercy (Ps. 103:8; 11 Chron. 30:9). It also describes Him as full of compassion and mercy (Jas. 5: 11).God's mercy is abundant, and that explains why He forbears with man the way He does. No man can see what God sees and still forbear with man. His mercies are very great (1 Chron. 21: 13). After considering the mercy of God, Faber (1847) wrote,

> No earthly father loves like Thee;
> No mother e'er so mild
> Bears and forbears as Thou had done
> With me Thy sinful child.

I think God kept parents from having full knowledge of their child's sinful thoughts and lifestyle in order to keep their love for him unaffected. Such knowledge will, no doubt, negatively impact on their love for the child, especially when the lifestyle persists defiantly. But God sees everything. He sees our most secret life and thoughts. They are bare to Him (Heb.

4:13). The Psalmist, David, was astounded when he considered the depth of God's knowledge of him. He declares in Psalm 139: 1-16:

[1]O LORD, you have searched me and you know me.

[2]You know when I sit and when I rise; you perceive my thoughts from afar.

[3]You discern my going out and my lying down; you are familiar with all my ways.

[4]Before a word is on my tongue you know it completely, O LORD.

[5]You hem me in—behind and before; you have laid your hand upon me.

[6]Such knowledge is too wonderful for me, too lofty for me to attain.

[7]Where can I go from your Spirit?

Where can I flee from your presence?

[8]If I go up to the heavens, you are there; if I make my bed in the depths, you are there.

[9]If I rise on the wings of the dawn, if I settle on the far side of the sea,

[10]even there your hand will guide me, your right hand will hold me fast.

[11]If I say, "Surely the darkness will hide me and the light become night around me,"

[12]even the darkness will not be dark to you; the night will shine like the day, for darkness is as light to you.

[13]For you created my inmost being; you knit me together in my mother's womb.

¹⁴I praise you because I am fearfully and wonderfully made; your works are wonderful, I know that full well.

¹⁵My frame was not hidden from you when I was made in the secret place.

When I was woven together in the depths of the earth,

¹⁶your eyes saw my unformed body.

All the days ordained for me were written in your book before one of them came to be.

Notice how, in awe, he declares in verse 6, "Such knowledge is too wonderful to me, too lofty for me to attain."

God watches people insult, deny, and blaspheme Him. He watches people worship idols rather than worship Him, commit murder and sexual immorality, cheat, lie, and do all kinds of evil. He watches people hatch wicked plans and execute them. The Bible says it is shameful even to mention what the disobedient do in secret (Eph. 5: 12). But God knows and sees them all. What man can endure such contempt? Yet God keeps forbearing with man. Why? His love is deeper than our sins, and He gives us time to repent (2 Peter 3: 9). In His love, He keeps extending His mercy to man and calling Him to come to Him despite his sin. He says, "Whoever comes to me I will never drive away" (John 6: 37); "though your sins be as scarlet, they shall be as white as snow; though they be red like crimson, they shall be as wool" (Is. 1:18); "Let the wicked forsake his way and the evil man his thoughts. Let him turn to the LORD, and he will have mercy on him, and to our God, for he will freely pardon" (Is. 55: 7). He is always ready to show mercy to anyone who turns to Him in repentance and faith. He is faithful and just to forgive us our sins and cleanse us from all unrighteousness when we confess our sins (1 Jn. 1: 9). What a merciful God!

Let us contrast His merciful heart with man's unforgiving spirit. A clear picture of the contrast is seen in the book of Jonah. Jonah was a man who feared the Lord (Jonah 1: 9, KJV), not a wicked man, yet his story clearly illustrates the difference between man's unforgiving spirit and God's large-mindedness. He could not put up with the wickedness of Nineveh for so long. He felt that Nineveh had gone beyond the point of mercy and should be judged and condemned. But God did not see it that way. God was still concerned about them and desired their repentance and salvation. He sent a word to Jonah to go and warn the people of Nineveh, but Jonah saw His heart in this and refused to go. He saw that God was offering mercy and not condemnation to the people, and he refused to be the instrument of the mercy. Instead, he boarded a ship to run to Tarshish. The Lord sent a great wind and a life-threatening storm to scare Jonah and get him to obey Him, but Jonah did not care. He knew that the raging storm came because of him, yet he refused to change his mind. He chose rather to die than live to see Nineveh forgiven. When the people in the ship found out he was the cause of the storm, rather than repent, he asked to be cast into the sea, but the mercy of God remained on him. He provided a fish that swallowed him and brought him to Nineveh after three days. Jonah then consented to go into Nineveh and warn them.

Following his warning, the people of Nineveh repented, from the greatest to the least of them, and God forgave them—the very thing that Jonah feared. He was exceedingly displeased. He now revealed why he never wanted to come to Nineveh on the mission in the first place. In bitterness, he prayed: "O LORD, is this not what I said when I was still at home? That is why I was quick to flee to Tarshish. I knew that you are a gracious and compassionate God, slow to anger and abounding in love, a God who relents from sending calamity. Now, O LORD, take away my life, for it is better for me to die than to live" (Jonah 4:2-3). He preferred dying to living to see Nineveh forgiven and spared the calamity they "so well deserved."

God's high tolerance level embittered Jonah. Is it not true that we sometimes feel the same way when we see a man we consider very wicked? We feel the only just thing for the person will be condemnation. We feel that it won't be fair for God to forgive him. We feel he is beyond forgiveness and wonder why he is still alive. You see, man has a very low tolerance limit, but God is slow to anger and abounding in mercy. In Romans 5: 8, the Scripture declares: "God demonstrates his own love for us in this: While we were still sinners, Christ died for us." Wow! You see again that His own love is deeper than our sins. He loved and cared for us even while we were still sinning and rebelling against Him. He continues to extend His mercy to us.

The love and mercy of God appear so lavish and unending. But there still comes a time when His mercy comes to an end. You may wonder how when the Bible says, "His mercy is everlasting . . ." (Psalm 100:5, NKJV). Yes, His mercy never comes to an end for people who received it in their lifetimes. It refers to those who have received His mercy in their lifetimes and who end up in heaven. It means that, at no time in all eternity will God change His mind and withdraw the mercy He has given them. His mercy, in this case, is forever. What then does it mean to say that there comes a time when His mercy comes to an end? When is this? Let us take a biblical illustration of what I am saying. In Luke 16: 19-31, Jesus told the story of Lazarus and the rich man. In that story, while in hell, the rich man pleaded for mercy. "Father Abraham," he said, "have mercy on me, and send Lazarus, that he may deep the tip of his finger in water, and cool my tongue; for I am tormented in this flame." But Abraham replied him saying, "Son, remember that in your lifetime you received your good things, while Lazarus received bad things, but now he is comforted here and you are in agony. And besides all this, between us and you a great chasm has been fixed, so that those who want to go from here to you cannot, nor can anyone cross over from there to us."

In that story, Abraham represented God and spoke His mind. The rich man's plea for mercy came when it was too late, and he did not get it. It tells me that there comes a time when God's mercy ends, when prayer is too late, and when repentance becomes useless. As long as one is alive on earth, God remains on His mercy seat for him and continues to extend His mercy to him, no matter his sin. But, once he breathes his last without accepting God's mercy, that's it. God descends from His mercy seat in regard to the individual and ascends His judgment seat. At that point, His mercy ends and His justice takes over. He passes His judgment, and that settles it. The person is cast into hell and doomed forever. Prayer for him, thenceforth, either by himself or any others, is useless. It cannot save him. In Heb. 9: 27 the Scripture says, "Man is destined to die once, and after that to face judgment." Once that judgment takes place, it is final and irreversible. The judgment also cannot be appealed against, for there is no higher authority to which one can appeal. More so, His judgment is just and perfect. No prayer can save the person; not even repentance can help him. At that point, repentance is too late and unacceptable, and God's mercy is no longer available for grabs. It is ended.

Abraham said to the rich man, "And besides all this, between us and you a great chasm has been fixed, so that those who want to go from here to you cannot, nor can anyone cross over from there to us" (v. 26). Who fixed the great chasm? God. Why? To make cross over from one to the other impossible.

Hence, the only time one has to access the mercy of God is while alive here on earth. Unfortunately, however, many people seek the mercy when it is no longer available. The Scripture admonishes: "Seek the Lord while he may be found; call on him while he is near" (Isaiah 55:6). This implies that there comes a time when He cannot be found and when He cannot hear a call. The time to seek and call Him is now that you still have the breath of life in you. Now is the day of salvation (2 Cor. 6:2), not tomorrow. Tomorrow may be too late. James 4: 13-14 says:

> Now listen, you who say, "Today or tomorrow we will go to this or that city, spend a year there, carry on business and make money." Why, you do not even know what will happen tomorrow. What is your life? You are a mist that appears for a little while and then vanishes.

Many of us procrastinate their repentance because they presume that there is always a tomorrow. They gloss over the brevity of life and by so doing, many have passed onto eternity without accepting God's mercy. In hell, they have repented like the rich man, but it is too late. They have sought the Lord when He could not be found and called on Him when He's too far and could not hear them. People go to hell not because they have sinned, for all have sinned (Rom. 3:23), but because they rejected God's mercy. They refused to repent and accept the payment Jesus has made for their sins on the cross of Calvary. They rejected Jesus and the forgiveness He secured for them. Only those who repent of their sins and believe in Jesus and the sacrifice He made for their sins have eternal life (Jn. 3:16; Jn. 1:12; Acts 2:38).

> **People go to hell not because they have sinned, for all have sinned (Rom. 3:23), but because they rejected God's mercy.**

How about you? Are you continuing in sin, hoping that you still have tomorrow to repent? Do not be deceived; there is no guarantee that you will have tomorrow. Some say, "I am still young. Let me enjoy myself now, and when I am old, I will repent." Others say, "When I get married, I will repent," or, "When I buy a car or buy a house, I will repent." Still others say, "When I'm done schooling, I will repent." James still asks, "Why, you do not even know what will happen tomorrow. What is your life? You are a mist that appears for a little while and then vanishes." You see, you cannot afford to procrastinate. You are only sure of now. Why not take advantage of it and secure your eternity? If God had made known to you when you will leave this earth, then you could afford to say, "Tomorrow, I will repent." But since God has not made this known to you, do you not think you need to be wise and make hay while the sun shines? I tell you the truth; you will miss nothing worthwhile by accepting God's mercy through repentance and faith in the Lord, Jesus Christ. Instead, you will be delivered from sin and its ugly consequences. You will gain righteousness, peace, and joy in the Holy Ghost (Rom. 14:17) and hereafter, life everlasting also. Right now, Jesus is saying to you, "Here I am! I stand at the door and knock. If anyone hears my voice and opens the door, I will come in and eat with him, and he with me" (Rev. 3:20). As you now hear his voice, once again, do not harden your heart (Heb. 3:15). He is gentle and will not force His way into your heart. He is standing at the door of your heart with mercy in His hands for you. Why not open the door for Him, be saved, and receive everlasting life. Ask Him in by faith and in genuine repentance. He will come in.

To you who have received the Lord's mercy already, I encourage you to remain in His grace. "Be very careful, then, how you live—not as unwise but as wise, making the most of every opportunity, because the days are evil. Therefore do not be foolish, but understand what the Lord's will is" (Eph. 5:15-17); "stand firm. Let nothing move you. Always give yourselves fully to the work of the Lord, because you know that your labor in the Lord is not in vain" (1 Cor. 15:58).

# Chapter Four

## The Folly of Pride

Pride is a feeling and attitude of superiority to others. It makes one perceive himself as bigger than he is. It puffs a person up and inflates his heart. It is an attitude of self-exaltation and glorification. A proud fellow considers himself above others and sees everyone else as under him. He is self-assertive and egocentric. He seeks to control and wants to be heard, feared, and obeyed. He is always right in his own eyes and is incorrigible. Pride always hinges on a perceived strength, real or imagined, of oneself. Such strengths could include good looks, talent, possession, position, background, etc. Pride makes people haughty and boastful. They boast about what they are, what they have, and what they do. They boast about their achievements. Indeed, it makes people play God. Pride makes people feel sufficient in themselves.

Pride is offensive to God. He hates pride (Prov. 8:13) because it gives people a false sense of self-worth. It makes people forget their frailty and ascribe to themselves the glory due God. In 1 Cor. 4: 7, the Scripture asks, "For who makes you different from anyone else? What do you have that you did not receive? And if you did receive it, why do you boast as though you did not?" The truth is: man did not make himself. The proud man forgets this. He forgets that he contributed nothing to his making; that he was born naked, possessing nothing, and that whatever appearance or abilities he possesses were given to him by his Maker. He grows up to discover that he has these gifts, and he foolishly begins to brag about them. He forgets how he was born into a world he knew nothing about and that does not belong to him. He forgets what a privilege it is for him to acquire anything therein. He forgets that since all he possesses was given to him by his Maker, they can also be taken away from him by his Maker. Man can lose whatever he possesses: beauty, talent, money, power, position, and even life. Pride makes a man forget that his life on earth generally is by grace. Truly, pride offends God so much as it is an insult to Him. In his right senses, man should tremble and worship his Maker, God, because he owes Him everything, even his life. He should recognize that whatever he has is not his, strictly speaking, he received it. He should therefore live in honor of the One who graciously gave it to him, being mindful of the fact that his continued possession of the gift depends on the Giver. He can choose to take it from him at any time. Indeed, life and everything it offers belong to God.

> **In his right senses, man should tremble and worship his Maker, God, because he owes Him everything, even his life.**

The Scripture says, "God resists the proud but gives grace to the humble" (Prov. 3:34, Jas. 4:6). The humble is one who recognizes his helplessness without God and who lives in submission and honor of Him; who uses his possessions for His glory. The proud man denies his Maker and lives in self-honor and glory. God resists such a man. Pride goes before destruction and a haughty spirit before a fall (Prov. 16: 18). It is a deceiver and gives one a false sense of security while blinding him to his imminent destruction. The Lord has this to say to those who have been deceived by it and who falsely feel secure: "The pride of your heart has deceived you, you who live in the clefts of the rocks and make your home on the heights, you who say to yourself, 'Who can bring me down to the ground?' Though you soar like the eagle and make your nest among the stars, from there I will bring you down" (Obadiah 1: 3-4).

> **The humble is one who recognizes his helplessness without God and who lives in submission and honor of Him; who uses his possessions for His glory.**

He has demonstrated this with some men who walked in pride. A few biblical examples will suffice to buttress the point. The book of Daniel tells the story of the king of Babylon named Nebuchadnezzar. In his time, he was the greatest and most powerful king in the whole world. God gave him dominion, power, might, and glory and placed in his hands mankind, the beasts of the field, and the birds of the air. He was the world ruler, and all nations dreaded and feared him (Dan. 2: 37-38; 5:19). But he was offensively proud. God warned him in a dream of the humiliation he was about to suffer. Daniel interpreted the dream to him and advised him to repent and seek God's mercy, but he would not listen. One year after, what God warned him against happened to him. One day, as he walked on the roof of the royal palace of Babylon, he proudly declared: "Is not this the great Babylon I have built as the royal residence, by my mighty power and for the glory of my majesty?" (Dan. 4: 30). Typical statement of a proud man, ascribing power and glory to himself: "Built . . . by my mighty power and for the glory of my majesty." "My" all the way. To the proud, life is all about "me' and "my"—very self-centered. Immediately, God decided to expose and humiliate him, and while he was still speaking, He sent a voice from heaven that said to him:

> This is what is decreed for you, King Nebuchadnezzar: Your royal authority has been taken from you. You will be driven away from people and will live with the wild animals; you will eat grass like cattle. Seven times will pass by for you until you acknowledge that the Most High is sovereign over the kingdoms of men and gives them to anyone he wishes (Dan. 4: 31-32).

Right away, everything the voice said happened to him. He was driven away from people, and he ate grass like cattle. More so, his body was drenched with the dew of heaven until his hair grew like the feathers of an eagle and his nails like the claws of a bird (v. 34). For seven years the king lived like a beast. At the end of the experience, he testified as follows:

> [34]At the end of that time, I, Nebuchadnezzar, raised my eyes toward heaven, and my sanity was restored. Then I praised the Most High; I honored and glorified him who lives forever. His dominion is an eternal dominion; his kingdom endures from generation to generation.
>
> [35]All the peoples of the earth are regarded as nothing.
>
> He does as he pleases with the powers of heaven and the peoples of the earth.
>
> No one can hold back his hand or say to him: "What have you done?"

<sup>36</sup>At the same time that my sanity was restored, my honor and splendor were returned to me for the glory of my kingdom. My advisers and nobles sought me out, and I was restored to my throne and became even greater than before. <sup>37</sup>Now I, Nebuchadnezzar, praise and exalt and glorify the King of heaven, because everything he does is right and all his ways are just. And those who walk in pride he is able to humble (Dan. 4: 34-37).

Notice his confession, "At the end of the time, I, Nebuchadnezzar, raised my eyes toward heaven . . . ," indicating surrender and acknowledgement of where his help would come from. He beckoned heaven for help. It was like saying, "I'm done!" He gave up himself and looked up for help. He took his eyes away from himself and looked up to heaven. And God had mercy and restored his sanity. Then he praised the Most High, honored and glorified Him who lives forever.

After the ordeal, he learned necessary lessons. He learned that the royal authority he had was given to him; he learned he could have been an animal save for the grace of God; he learned that his wisdom was a gift to him; he learned to honor and glorify God; he learned that God is sovereign over the kingdoms of men and gives them to whomever He wills; and he learned that God is able to humble those who walk in pride. These are lessons for us all. Notice that God restored him to his position and made him even greater after teaching him those lessons. One soars higher with humility.

Surprisingly, as is usual with men, his son Belshazzar, who succeeded him as king, did not learn from his father's experience. He needed to be taught his own lesson. Unfortunately, his was more devastating, and he could not live to share it (Dan. 5). He gave a feast for a thousand of his nobles. He gave orders that the gold and silver goblets that Nebuchadnezzar his father had taken from the temple of God in Jerusalem be brought in. The king, his nobles, wives, and concubines ate and drank from the goblets. Contemptuously, as they drank from the goblets from the Lord's temple, they praised the gods of gold and silver, of bronze, iron, wood, and stone.

Suddenly, God, in anger, caused a human hand to appear and to write on the plaster of the wall near the lampstand in the royal palace. The king watched the hand as it wrote, and he was utterly perplexed and melted away in fear. The Scripture describes it thus: "His face turned pale and he was so frightened that his knees knocked together and his legs gave way" (v. 6). And I ask, "O king, where is your power? Where is your might? Why are you afraid?" You see the frailty of man and the folly of pride. Here is a man who, a moment ago, basked in glory and power and paraded himself as all in all before his noble, wives, and concubines, now trembling and wobbling at the sight of a mere hand writing on the wall. All his self-sufficiency vanished instantly, exposing his helplessness. He could not hide his fear from those before whom he displayed his glory. If only man would realize how powerless he is, he would tremble and worship the Almighty God. The king summoned all the enchanters, astrologers, and diviners of Babylon to have them read and interpret the writing, but none could do that. None could until Daniel, the servant of the living God, was invited. In anger, Daniel reminded the king of his father Nebuchadnezzar's experience and then added:

> "But you his son, O Belshazzar, have not humbled yourself, though you knew all this. Instead, you have set yourself up against the Lord of heaven. You had the goblets from his temple

brought to you, and you and your nobles, your wives and your concubines drank wine from them. You praised the gods of silver and gold, of bronze, iron, wood and stone, which cannot see or hear or understand. But you did not honor the God who holds in his hand your life and all your ways. Therefore he sent the hand that wrote the inscription.

"This is the inscription that was written:
Mene, Mene, Tekel, Parsin
"This is what these words mean:
Mene: God has numbered the days of your reign and brought it to an end.
Tekel: You have been weighed on the scales and found wanting.
Peres: Your kingdom is divided and given to the Medes and Persians" (Dan. 5: 22-28).

That very night, King Belshazzar was slain, and Darius the Mede took over, as the Lord said. Pity!

A proud man, indeed, foolishly sets himself up against God who holds his life and his ways in His hand. He is like the little bird, *nza*, in the Igbo adage, who challenges his god to a wrestling bout after a heavy meal. Folly!

There is yet another man in the Scripture I will not fail to talk about. His name was Herod, also a king (Acts 12: 20-23). He had a quarrel with the people of Tyre and Sidon who depended on his country for their food supply. The people of the two countries joined together and sought audience with him for peace. On the appointed day, Herod dressed in his royal robes, sat on his throne, and delivered a public address to the people. In awe, the people shouted, "This is the voice of a god, not of a man" (v.22). And the Scripture says, "Immediately, because

Herod did not give praise to God, an angel of the Lord struck him down, and he was eaten by warms and died" (v. 23).

Herod took the glory due God and God publicly reduced him to nothing he was. Man is but dust (Gen. 2:7; 3:19). He is just an earthen vessel that God uses. Of his own, he can do nothing (John 15:5). God infuses His power into man and enables him to work, and man turns around to challenge God. Utter foolishness! But that is what pride makes man do. Lest we forget, it was the same pride that brought Satan down from heaven. He was an exalted and powerful angel, but he became proud and wanted to rub shoulders with the Most High. See what his fate became as a result (Isaiah 14:12-15):

---

**Man is but dust (Gen. 2:7; 3:19). He is just an earthen vessel that God uses. Of his own, he can do nothing (John 15:5).**

---

¹²How you have fallen from heaven, O morning star, son of the dawn! You have been cast down to the earth, you who once laid low the nations!

¹³You said in your heart,
"I will ascend to heaven;
I will raise my throne above the stars of God;
I will sit enthroned on the mount of assembly,
on the utmost heights of the sacred mountain.

¹⁴I will ascend above the tops of the clouds;
I will make myself like the Most High."

¹⁵But you are brought down to the grave, to the depths of the pit.

Pride brings down.

If only man will be wise and understand the goodness of God. God intends to use man to accomplish His purposes. He provides the strength and is willing to do the work using us. If any vessel submits himself to Him, He uses him and at the end blesses him. Thus, He says, if you are willing and obedient, talking about our yieldedness, you will eat the best of the land (Is. 1:19). We do nothing except to yield ourselves to Him. He fills us with His awesome power, uses us, and turns around and blesses us for it. Isn't that amazing?

King David was a man who understood the greatness of God. As he pondered His awesome greatness, man paled into utter insignificance in comparison. He wrote:

> ¹O LORD, our Lord, how majestic is your name in all the earth!
> You have set your glory above the heavens.
> ³When I consider your heavens, the work of your fingers, the moon and the stars, which you have set in place,
> ⁴what is man that you are mindful of him, the son of man that you care for him? (Ps. 8:1, 3-4).

No wonder he was such a humble man—a man who acknowledged God in all his ways and who depended solely on Him. He pleased God so much that God described him as a man after His own heart (I Sam. 13:14, Acts 13:22) and esteemed him above all the kings of Israel. David is a shining example for us to follow.

Sometimes, when a man finds himself excelling in some areas of life, he tends to think he achieved it. He attributes his excellence to his brilliance, power, or might, hard work, cleverness, or connections. He forgets that "it is not of him that willeth, nor of him that runneth, but of God that sheweth mercy" (Rom. 9:16, KJV). He forgets that the race is not to the swift, nor yet riches to men of understanding, nor favor to men of skill; but that time and chance happen to them all (Ecc. 9:11). Who is behind time and chance? God, of course. One also forgets the eternal truth declared by Solomon in Psalm 127:1-2:

> [1]Unless the LORD builds the house, its builders labor in vain.
> Unless the LORD watches over the city, the watchmen stand guard in vain.
> [2]In vain you rise early and stay up late, toiling for food to eat . . .
> God is all in all.

I recall how the Lord taught me how helpless and powerless I am without Him to keep me from boasting. I had a smooth ride from primary through secondary school to the university. I obtained a bachelor's degree in economics and an MBA in banking and finance at a relatively young age from a renowned university in Nigeria. And this was at a time of proliferation of high-paying merchant banks in the country that were looking for young people, twenty-seven years and under, who held MBA degrees. I felt well positioned for a high flying job in a merchant bank, and I was already seeing myself flying high. Moreover, I had so many connections that would ensure my getting one of those jobs. But God saw my heart. He saw that if I moved that way, my head would be swollen, and I would think it was my cleverness and multitude of connections that achieved it for me. He saw that I would feel wiser than my mates and would despise others who were not as privileged. Consequently, He made sure that nothing worked out for me. At a time, I decided to leave the country for greener pastures. I tried exploiting the connection of my brothers who were in the United States of America, but God also frustrated all my efforts in that direction. For over four years, I was jobless. I lost every confidence in myself and fell like a pack of cards, exhausted. I came to the end of myself. Then I learned the eternal lesson in Psalm 33:16-18:

> No king is saved by the size of his army; no warrior escapes by his great strength. A horse is a vain hope for deliverance; despite all its great strength it cannot save. But the eyes of the LORD are on those who fear him, on those whose hope is in his unfailing love.

I realized that apart from God, I could do nothing. I learned that my degrees and multitude of human connections could not help me apart from God. God emptied me of myself and of everything I could pride myself in, and I acknowledged my emptiness. I then declared like Paul, "My sufficiency is of God" (2 Cor. 3:5). It was at that point that He knew I could now walk with Him and not take His glory. God does not ever want to share His glory with any man (Is. 42:8). He then picked me up and began to help me again. Now, I tremble at whatever position I find myself in and concerning whatever virtue I find in myself and declare: "It is God!" And when I say it, I mean it.

The truth is, when God gives you any gift, He means it for the good of mankind, your blessing, and His glory ultimately. In fact, He created you for His glory and pleasure (Is. 43:7; Rev. 4:11). We owe Him our whole lives.

> **The truth is, when God gives you any gift, He means it for the good of mankind, your blessing, and His glory ultimately.**

Do you find yourself possessing any gift? Count it a privilege, acknowledge the Giver, and use it in His honor. He will not only sustain it, He will increase it. Remember, God is sovereign. He gives grace to the humble and opposes the proud (Jas. 4:6). Therefore, humble yourself before Him, and He will exalt you (Matt. 23:12).

# Chapter Five

## Run to Win

When Jesus completed His earthly ministry, before he ascended into heaven, He left His disciples with one great commission: go and preach the gospel to all nations. Two of the gospel books recorded the great commission as Jesus's final charge to His disciples. In Matthew 28: 18-20, Jesus tells them:

> "All authority in heaven and on earth has been given to me. Therefore go and make disciples of all nations, baptizing them in the name of the Father and of the Son and of the Holy Spirit, and teaching them to obey everything I have commanded you. And surely I am with you always, to the very end of the age."

Mark 16: 15-16 puts it thus:

> And He said to them, "Go into all the world and preach the gospel to every creature. He who

believes and is baptized will be saved; but he who does not believe will be condemned.

Jesus promised to empower them with the Holy Spirit for the task (Lk 24:49; Acts 1: 4, 5, 8). He fulfilled the promise on the day of Pentecost by filling them with the Holy Spirit with the result that they preached the gospel powerfully, and about three thousand people were added to their number (Acts 2).

Jesus would have taken his disciples with Him back to heaven, but He did not. He left them behind for the one reason of preaching the gospel to all nations—an enormous task. The gospel is about what Jesus has done for mankind—the redemption He has brought to the world. He came and paid the price for the sin of mankind by His death on the cross. By His shed blood, Christ satisfied the condition for the remission of sins for mankind. Consequently, in Christ, God was reconciling the world to Himself, not counting men's sins against them, but forgiving them (2 Cor. 5:19). If any man therefore believes in the sacrifice of Jesus, he shall not perish but have everlasting life (Jn. 3:16). God needed to take the good news of man's redemption from sin and condemnation to mankind all over the world. That is what Jesus commissioned His disciples to do so that man will embrace the salvation that has been secured for them. That is why He left them behind when He ascended into heaven. The assignment is urgent and compelling because it is about saving of lives in danger of eternal destruction. He empowered them for it, and these men were committed to the task. Their effort is why we are believers today. Those men are no longer with us, but the work is yet to be completed. They played their part and handed the baton over to us to see to the completion of the job. It is like a relay race, and we must complete our assigned leg timely. We should therefore know it as believers that the primary reason we are still on earth is to preach the gospel to all nations. Every believer should realize this and be committed to the commission. Hence, our primary goal in everything we do should be to preach the gospel and win souls for the Lord. Anything short of this amounts to unfaithfulness. Our goal in everything should be like Paul's: "that I might by all means save some," (I Cor. 9:22). Thus, in business and at play, in leisure and at work, and in all our interactions with people, our target should be to win souls thereby. That should be our primary goal. Whatever other goal of that task is secondary. We should do whatever in the name of the Lord and for His glory (1 Cor. 10:31, Col. 3:17). That way, men may see our good works and glorify our Father who is in heaven (Matthew 5:16). Our whole life should call attention to God. We should be mission-minded.

> **We should therefore know it as believers that the primary reason we are still on earth is to preach the gospel to all nations.**

Paul was one man who understood his mission as a believer and who pursued it with everything in him. We will do well to look at his example. In 1 Cor. 9:16, he emphatically declared: "Woe to me if I do not preach the gospel!" He then outlined his strategy in verses 19-23 of the same chapter:

> [19]Though I am free and belong to no man, I make myself a slave to everyone, to win as many as possible.
>
> [20]To the Jews I became like a Jew, to win the Jews. To those under the law I became like one under the law (though I myself am not under the law), so as to win those under the law.

> **In business and at play, in leisure and at work, and in all our interactions with people, our target should be to win souls thereby. That should be our primary goal. Whatever other goal of that task is secondary.**

²¹To those not having the law I became like one not having the law (though I am not free from God's law but am under Christ's law), so as to win those not having the law.

²²To the weak I became weak, to win the weak. I have become all things to all men so that by all possible means I might save some.

²³I do all this for the sake of the gospel, that I may share in its blessings.

I see passion and focus in those statements. I see a man consumed by passion for his mission and a man so focused that he wouldn't be distracted. Let's get him right, he did not mean he was ready to compromise with sin. No! He interacted with people with focus on his goal—the goal of winning some. Such a man cannot compromise with sin, as he was not careless. He was following his Master's example. Jesus had to become man in order to reach man. But becoming man, He did not become a sinner with man. He only became one of us to save us. While on earth, Jesus ate with sinners with a view to winning them, but He did not compromise with sin. When He ate with Matthew and Zaccheus, who were tax collectors and sinners, the Scribes and Pharisees criticized Him, but He won both men to Himself (Matt. 9:10-11, Lk. 19:5-7). He neither joined them to sin nor encouraged them to sin; instead, He turned them from it. He said He came to call sinners to repentance (Lk. 5:32). He interacted with them with a view to save them from their sin. That was Paul's strategy, too—contact without contamination.

---

**Jesus had to become man in order to reach man. But becoming man, He did not become a sinner with man. He only became one of us to save us.**

---

That reminds me of the testimony shared by a pastor, of how they evangelized a primitive river community many years ago. Dressed in the normal attire of the civilized world, the people of the community rejected them and would not listen to them. They went home unsuccessful. In their second visit to the community, they dressed like them—half-naked—and the community welcomed them, and they reaped a rich harvest of souls for Christ. I am also reminded of an experience during my national youth service year in 1989. The Christian corpers's fellowship had an evangelistic outreach to a community in Oyo state, Nigeria. On arrival, we carried out some sensitization programs to attract the villagers, but, surprisingly, they mocked at us and wouldn't pay attention to us. Consequently, our first night's program in the community was a total failure. On inquiry, we were informed that their response was because our ladies wore trousers. To the community, trousers were for men, and women who wore trousers were regarded as irresponsible and wayward. They therefore considered us not genuine and laughed at us. Our ladies actually wore a corpers's paramilitary uniform, which included trousers both for ladies and gentlemen. We all wore our uniforms for identification purposes so as to be accepted, but it backfired. The community simply interpreted our ladies' appearance as strange and an aberration for religious women. When we learned this, we asked all our ladies to change and dress in gowns, skirts, and wrappers for the rest of the days' programs, and we were welcomed and the outreach turned out a huge success. We learned our lesson, and in all our subsequent outreaches to villages, our ladies never wore trousers, and we never had any problem of acceptance again. That is what is meant by becoming all things to all men so as to win some.

Paul likened his mission, and indeed our mission, to a race and committed himself, even his life, to finishing it (Acts 20:24). As he forged ahead in the race, he faced terrible challenges: suffering and persecution. In 2 Cor. 11:23-29, he encapsulated his ordeal in the cause of preaching the gospel as follows:

> [23]I have worked much harder, been in prison more frequently, been flogged more severely, and been exposed to death again and again.
>
> [24]Five times I received from the Jews the forty lashes minus one.
>
> [25]Three times I was beaten with rods, once I was stoned, three times I was shipwrecked, I spent a night and a day in the open sea,
>
> [26]I have been constantly on the move. I have been in danger from rivers, in danger from bandits, in danger from my own countrymen, in danger from Gentiles; in danger in the city, in danger in the country, in danger at sea; and in danger from false brothers.
>
> [27]I have labored and toiled and have often gone without sleep; I have known hunger and thirst and have often gone without food; I have been cold and naked.
>
> [28]Besides everything else, I face daily the pressure of my concern for all the churches.
>
> [29]Who is weak, and I do not feel weak? Who is led into sin, and I do not inwardly burn?

More so, he added that the Holy Spirit testified in every city, saying that chains and tribulations awaited him (Acts 20:23). To all these, Paul responded: "But none of these things move me; nor do I count my life dear to myself, so that I may finish my race with joy, and the ministry which I received from the Lord Jesus, to testify to the gospel of the grace of God" (Acts 20:24). From prison he wrote to the Philippian church of his "earnest expectation and hope that in nothing I shall be ashamed, but with all boldness, as always, so now also Christ will be magnified in my body, whether by life or by death. For to me, to live is Christ, and to die is gain" (Phil. 1:20-21).

Paul's ministry was not all about suffering, nevertheless. He also achieved tremendous successes. God performed great miracles by him—healing the sick and casting out demons. He also received awesome revelations—caught up to the third heaven and told unspeakable things (2 Cor. 12:2-3); and he planted so many churches including the churches in Corinth, Rome, Galatia, Ephesus, Philippi, Colosse, and Thessalonica— achievements that could swell a man's head. But neither his sufferings nor his achievements meant anything to him. He was not ready to rest on his laurels. He still said:

> [12]Not that I have already obtained all this, or have already been made perfect, but I press on to take hold of that for which Christ Jesus took hold of me.
>
> [13]Brothers, I do not consider myself yet to have taken hold of it. But one thing I do: Forgetting what is behind and straining toward what is ahead,
>
> [14]I press on toward the goal to win the prize for which God has called me heavenward in Christ Jesus (Phil. 3:12-14).

He knew the race was not over yet despite what he had suffered for the gospel and what he had accomplished for Christ. He kept his eyes on the ultimate prize of the race—heaven and crown of righteousness. He kept running and fighting. He challenged and inspired the Corinthian church with these words:

> $^{24}$Do you not know that in a race all the runners run, but only one gets the prize? Run in such a way as to get the prize.
>
> $^{25}$Everyone who competes in the games goes into strict training. They do it to get a crown that will not last; but we do it to get a crown that will last forever.
>
> $^{26}$Therefore I do not run like a man running aimlessly; I do not fight like a man beating the air.
>
> $^{27}$No, I beat my body and make it my slave so that after I have preached to others, I myself will not be disqualified for the prize (1 Cor. 9: 24-27).

With those words, he challenged them to be determined and disciplined while targeting the prize. Paul is saying that if athletes who compete for a perishable crown subject themselves to such strict training as they do, Christians should do more who compete for imperishable crown. This calls for wisdom on the part of all of us who believe. He says we should run with a purpose, not as one running aimlessly or one beating the air. He warns of the danger of complacency—the danger of being disqualified. This is consistent with what he told Timothy in 2 Timothy 2:3-7:

³Endure hardship with us like a good soldier of Christ Jesus.

⁴No one serving as a soldier gets involved in civilian affairs—he wants to please his commanding officer.

⁵Similarly, if anyone competes as an athlete, he does not receive the victor's crown unless he competes according to the rules.

⁶The hardworking farmer should be the first to receive a share of the crops.

⁷Reflect on what I am saying, for the Lord will give you insight into all this.

Paul is highlighting the need to focus and avoid distraction—not get entangled with civilian affairs; the need to run according to rules (the biblical standards) and the need to work hard. Paul was committed to running well and finishing the race. He kept his eyes on the prize, which surpasses all the sufferings of the race. As he says, "Our present sufferings are not worth comparing with the glory that will be revealed in us" (Rom. 8:18). Again he says, "We do not lose heart. Though outwardly we are wasting away, yet inwardly we are being renewed day by day. For our light and momentary troubles are achieving for us an eternal glory that far outweighs them all" (2 Cor. 4: 16-17). Inspired by this hope, he persevered to the end, and in 2 Timothy 4:6-8 he finally declared:

⁶For I am already being poured out like a drink offering, and the time has come for my departure.

⁷I have fought the good fight, I have finished the race, I have kept the faith.

<sup>8</sup>Now there is in store for me the crown of righteousness, which the Lord, the righteous Judge, will award to me on that day—and not only to me, but also to all who have longed for his appearing.

What an example and a challenge to us.

Paul's example is very like that of our Lord, Jesus Christ. In John 4:34, Jesus defined His mission thus: "My food is to do the will of him who sent me and to finish his work." God the Father was the one who sent Him. His work was the salvation of mankind. The salvation was to be accomplished by Jesus's death on the cross. Right from childhood, Jesus prepared Himself for the task and studied His program. From the inception of His ministry, He demonstrated focus, commitment, determination, and discipline. On the day He revealed His mission and passion as we saw it above, He had worked and journeyed for a long time and was tired and hungry (John 4). He sat down by Jacob's well in a Samaritan town called Sychar while His disciples went into town to buy food. A Samaritan woman came by to draw water from the well, presenting an opportunity for Jesus to save a soul. Tired and hungry as he was, Jesus grabbed the opportunity. He initiated a conversation with her geared toward saving her life. Eventually, he succeeded. When His disciples came back with food and urged Him to eat some, He said to them, "I have food to eat that you know nothing about" (Jn. 4:32). His disciples wondered whether someone had brought Him food while they were away. But he said to them, "My food is to do the will of him who sent me and to finish his work . . ." (v. 34). Awesome!

Actually, Jesus was tired and hungry, and His disciples knew it. He needed food for refreshment and energy. But once He saw an opportunity to save a life, His passion for souls spurred

Him on and supplied the needed energy. After accomplishing the task of saving the soul, the joy of that accomplishment refreshed and satisfied Him, and He had no need for food. Hence, He would not eat the food provided by the disciples.

Jesus remained focused and passionate about His mission. He allowed nothing to distract Him—not fame, nor riches, nor glory, nor suffering, nor anything else. He faced diverse temptations but wouldn't yield for even a second. Satan tempted Him and offered Him all the kingdoms of the world and their glory if only He would bow down and worship him, but He responded, "Away from me Satan! For it is written: 'Worship the Lord your God and serve him only'" (Matt. 4: 8-10). Satan meant to deceive Him into abandoning His mission and chasing the riches of the world and the glory thereof—what he has used to deceive many ministers of the gospel today. But Jesus turned down the offer.

Again, after Peter revealed the identity of Jesus as the Messiah, Jesus began to talk about His impending suffering and death. Satan entered Peter and by him took Jesus apart and rebuked Him for talking about suffering. Satan wanted to distract Him by making Him see Himself as an all-powerful and glorious Messiah devoid of the cross. But Jesus saw beyond Peter and said to him, "Get behind me Satan! You are a stumbling block to me; you do not have in mind the things of God, but the things of men" (Matt. 16:23). Thus, He remained focused.

After a time, Jesus became very famous. After feeding five thousand men with just five loaves of bread and two small fish, the crowd wanted to make Him king by force. When He realized this, He withdrew to a mountain by Himself (Jn. 6: 1-15). Again, He revealed His lack of interest in earthly kingdoms.

When He was approaching His crucifixion, the agony of the cross came over Him. He wished the cup could be taken away from Him and prayed as such. His anguish was too great that His sweat was like drops of blood falling to the ground (Lk. 22:44), but He still yielded to the sovereign will of God, declaring: "Yet not as I will, but as you will" (Matt. 26: 39). While He was being crucified, He remained focused in a way that continues to amaze me. While He was right on the cross being beaten and mocked, the Bible says, He knew that all was now completed, and so that the Scripture would be fulfilled, He said, "I am thirsty" (Jn. 19:28). It shows that despite the pain He was bearing and the commotion of the time, he was still focused on fulfilling what the Scripture said about Him to the letter. He was still mindful of doing the will of Him who sent Him and was still committed to finishing His work. He was still thinking of the next word to fulfill. The pain and torture were justifiable reason for anybody in His shoes to forget the minute details of what comes next, but not so for Jesus. He still remembers what comes next and was not ready to stop short of perfect obedience. He called out, "I am thirsty" in order to elicit the only one thing that remained for Him to complete His assignment. They soaked a sponge in a jar of wine vinegar and lifted it to His lips. When He received the drink, He knew that there was absolutely nothing outstanding for Him to fulfill. Then He announced: "It is finished" (Jn. 19: 30), implying, "I have completed my assignment—it is finished! Done!" With that, He bowed down His head and gave up His spirit. Wow!

The Scripture reveals that one thing that kept Him going was the joy awaiting Him in heaven. The Scripture says He endured the cross and scorned its shame for the sake of the joy set before Him. Today, He is sitting at the right hand of the throne of God (Heb. 12:2). The prize set before Him spurred Him on, and He passionately pursued His mission and faithfully accomplished it. He ran to win, and He won.

Jesus left us an example by the way He ran that we may follow in His steps. Jesus was faithful to the one who appointed

Him, and the Scripture urges us to fix our thoughts on Him (Heb. 3:1-2). Also, in Hebrews 12: 1-2, the Scripture mobilizes us with these words, "Let us lay aside every weight, and the sin which doth so easily beset us, and let us run with patience the race that is set before us, looking unto Jesus the author and finisher of our faith; who for the joy that was set before him endured the cross, despising the shame, and is set down at the right hand of the throne of God. For consider him that endured such contradiction of sinners against himself, lest ye be wearied and faint in your minds." God encourages us to run light, free of all encumbrances such as dirty habits, bad company, lust of the flesh, lust of the eyes, pride of life, and other besetting sins. Those things hinder our movement. They are weights and must be cast overboard. He exhorts us to keep in focus the joy that is set before us in Christ just as Jesus did and run with perseverance the race that is marked out for us. He admonishes that we should not be discouraged by oppositions of men, but should consider how Jesus, who knew no sin, endured the opposition of sinful men. He assures us of a glorious position and crown in heaven. He wants us to run to the end—to finish the race. The apostle Paul followed Jesus's example studiously and thus stands as an outstanding challenge to us. All the apostles of Jesus followed the example too.

Some men in history also picked up the challenge and sacrificed their lives for the cause of spreading the gospel. Men like David Livingstone, the missionary who explored the continent of Africa with the gospel. A medical doctor regarded as the pathfinder of Africa, he dedicated his life to the cause of taking the gospel to the dark continent of Africa. When invited back to the comfort and opportunities of the civilized world, he answered, "I am a missionary, heart and soul. God had an only Son, and He was a missionary and a physician. I am a poor, poor imitation of Him, or wish to be. In this service I hope to live; in it I wish to die!" True to his commitment, he lived entirely in the service and died in it on his knees in Africa.

Men like Raymund Lull, the first missionary to the Mohammedans (1290-1315). This man inherited a large wealth from his father but sold all his property and gave all to the poor, leaving just enough for his wife and children to maintain a simple lifestyle. He attacked Islam frontally with the sword of Truth at a time when Islam was the greatest power in the world and claimed more political influence. He preached powerfully in North Africa, the stronghold of Mohammedanism, and defied imprisonment and banishment from the region. With great zeal, he continued to preach to people who persecuted him until he was seized, dragged out of town, and stoned to death at the age of eighty.

Men like William Carey, an English Baptist missionary to India. A shoemaker turned a missionary and scholar; he was responsible for the formation of a Baptist Missionary Society for propagating the gospel among the heathen. He is regarded as the father of modern missions. For forty years he labored and toiled for the gospel in India, including translating the Scriptures. A self-made scholar and linguist, he mastered Greek and Hebrew languages without a teacher. He learned other languages and could read the Bible in as many as six languages apart from English: Latin, Greek, Hebrew, Dutch, Italian, and French. Before he died, he had seen Scriptures translated in forty different languages and 212,000 copies of them printed by the Mission Press and sent out among hundred millions of people. He also became a college professor and founded a college at Serampore and had seen India open its doors to missionaries. He saw the edict passed prohibiting sati (burning widows on the funeral pyres of their dead husbands); and he saw Indian converts for Christ. On his deathbed, Carey said to a missionary friend, "Dr. Duff! You have been speaking about Dr. Carey; when I am gone, say nothing about Dr. Carey—speak about Dr. Carey's God." Great! These men were gospel heroes.

Lack of time will prevent me from talking about David Brainerd—missionary to the Indians at twenty-four; Samuel Crowther—the slave boy who became a bishop; Robert Morrison—founder of protestant missions in China; Adoniram Judson—missionary to Burma; Fidelia Fiske—first unmarried woman to go to Persia as a missionary; and a host of others (Johnston 2001).

We can also play a vital role in the spread of the gospel by supporting missionaries with our resources and praying fervently for them.

We should pick up courage and determination, renew our commitment to Christ and the gospel, refocus, discipline ourselves, and persevere in the race. It is a race for life and the command is: Don't look back, and don't stop anywhere! No retreat, no surrender! Run with the gospel! Spread it! Run to the finish line! Run to win! Jesus says, "No one, having put his hand on the plow and looking back, is fit for the kingdom of God (Lk 9:62). God says:

> [35]So do not throw away your confidence; it will be richly rewarded.
> [36]You need to persevere so that when you have done the will of God, you will receive what he has promised.
> [37]For in just a very little while,
> "He who is coming will come and will not delay.
> [38]But my righteous one will live by faith.
> And if he shrinks back,
> I will not be pleased with him" (Heb. 10:35-38).

Therefore, my beloved brethren, be steadfast, immovable, always abounding in the work of the Lord, knowing that your labor is not in vain in the Lord (1 Cor. 15: 35, NKJV).

An awesome reward awaits us in heaven. And by faith I declare that we are not of those who draw back unto perdition, but of those who believe and are saved, for we are more than conquerors through Christ Jesus our Lord.(Heb. 10: 39; Rom. 8:37). Amen!

# Chapter Six

## Victory Through Praise

The devil hates to see man have and enjoy a relationship with God. He will do everything to see it does not happen. When he sees any such relationship anywhere, he fights to sever it. His anger is borne out of frustration, envy, and jealousy. He was an exalted angel who lost his position and place in heaven. Having been in heaven, he knows the glory thereof; and having lost it, he does not want to see anyone else inherit it. He is an example of one having a reprobate mind. Knowing his doom—hell—he wants to take as many people as possible with him. He knows that God means to give His kingdom to man (Lk 12:32), and he detests the plan. Consequently, he fights day and night to ensure that man does not inherit the kingdom of heaven. He is ferocious in this battle. He has three agendas: to steal, kill, and destroy (Jn 10:10). God has revealed this, so we know. He is the enemy of our souls.

The devil employs various weapons in his battle to ensure that man does not develop a relationship with God. He tries to sever any existing relationship between man and God and destroy man. He employs deception, temptation, and affliction including rejection, sickness, hardship, and threat of death, among others.

Interestingly, God has given us various ways of dealing with and defeating the devil. Ephesians 6:10-18 summarizes the weapons of our warfare and urges us to put on the whole armor of God so that we can take our stand against the devil's schemes. The list includes: the belt of truth, the breastplate of righteousness, the gospel of peace, the shield of faith, the helmet of salvation, the sword of the Spirit, which is the word of God, and prayer.

In this message, we want to highlight one way of application of our defensive weapon, the shield of faith, which terribly disarms and frustrates the devil. That aspect is praise—praising God under adversity. Have you ever found yourself in a position where you were saying something you considered important, and somebody was busy laughing at you? How did you feel? That is exactly how the devil feels when believers praise in the face of afflictions he brings on them. The picture is that the devil is busy furiously attacking the believer, and the believer goes on smiling and praising God. As the devil intensifies his attack, the believer carries on with smiles and praise—the last thing the devil expects at the time. Can you imagine his frustration? To clarify this point, we will need to see some biblical examples.

A good example from the Old Testament was Job (Job 1). Job lived in the land of Uz and was the greatest man among all the people of the East. He was very wealthy; he had seven sons and three daughters and owned seven thousand sheep, three thousand camels, five hundred yoke of oxen, and five hundred donkeys. He also had a large number of servants. Job was also said to be a man of integrity who feared God and shunned evil. One day, Satan afflicted him terribly with a view to have him curse God to His face. That is usually what he wants to achieve when he afflicts us. He wants us to lose faith in God and tell

Him off. On a particular day, in one swoop, Satan destroyed all that Job owned. See how the Scripture reported it:

> <sup>13</sup>One day when Job's sons and daughters were feasting and drinking wine at the oldest brother's house,
>
> <sup>14</sup>a messenger came to Job and said, "The oxen were plowing and the donkeys were grazing nearby,
>
> <sup>15</sup>and the Sabeans attacked and carried them off. They put the servants to the sword, and I am the only one who has escaped to tell you!"
>
> <sup>16</sup>While he was still speaking, another messenger came and said, "The fire of God fell from the sky and burned up the sheep and the servants, and I am the only one who has escaped to tell you!"
>
> <sup>17</sup>While he was still speaking, another messenger came and said, "The Chaldeans formed three raiding parties and swept down on your camels and carried them off. They put the servants to the sword, and I am the only one who has escaped to tell you!"
>
> <sup>18</sup>While he was still speaking, yet another messenger came and said, "Your sons and daughters were feasting and drinking wine at the oldest brother's house,
>
> <sup>19</sup>when suddenly a mighty wind swept in from the desert and struck the four corners of the house. It collapsed on them and they are dead, and I am the only one who has escaped to tell you!" (Job 1:13-19).

Can you imagine such a sweeping attack on a man? Can you imagine a man receiving such tragic news all at the same time? Thunderous and devastating! Such news can crush a man. It was deathly grievous.

The Scripture says that Job got up, tore his robe, and shaved his head—expressions of pain and agony. I can imagine the devil smiling and saying to himself, I knew it, as he watched Job do this. Next thing, Job fell to the ground. Of course, virtually anybody would. Some people might collapse and die immediately. Job fell to the ground, but contrary to Satan's expectation, he worshipped God. Awesome! He said:

> "Naked I came from my mother's womb, and naked I will depart.
> The LORD gave and the LORD has taken away; may the name of the LORD be praised" (Job 1:20).

I believe this gave Satan the shocker of his life. He was expecting that as Job opened his mouth while on the ground, he would question God's whereabouts when all these happened and curse Him to His face in frustration and bitterness. But rather Job appreciated God's sovereignty in giving and in taking those things and praised the name of the Lord. And the Scripture concluded that Job did not sin by charging God with wrongdoing in all this. Thus, the devil's plan to have him curse God failed. Job overcame through praise.

Another interesting testimony of victory through praise is found in 2 Chronicles 20. The Moabites and Ammonites, along with some Meunites, came to make war on Jehoshaphat, King of Judah. Jehoshaphat inquired of the Lord and received assurance of victory from Him. He believed God. Early the next morning, Jehoshaphat mobilized his people for battle. As they set out, he said to them, "Listen to me, Judah and people of Jerusalem! Have faith in the Lord your God and you will be upheld; have faith in His prophets and you will be successful" (v.20). He then appointed men to sing to the Lord and praise Him for the splendor of His holiness as they went out before the army, saying: "Give thanks to the LORD, for his love endures forever" (v. 21).

As they began to sing and praise, the Lord sent ambushes against the invading armies, and they were defeated. The armies turned against one another and destroyed themselves. Jehoshaphat and his army simply went in and carried off their plunder. Amazing!

Yet another great example worth mentioning was that of Paul and Silas in the Philippian prison (Acts 16:16-40). After delivering a demon-possessed slave girl who made money for her owners through fortune-telling, the owners had them arrested and brought before magistrates. They were falsely accused of throwing the city into an uproar by advocating unlawful customs. The magistrates ordered that they be stripped, beaten, and put in prison. They were severely flogged and cast into prison where their feet were fastened in the stocks. About midnight, Paul and Silas prayed and sang hymns to God and the other prisoners listened to them. Consider their condition: these were men in terrible pain following a thorough beating they just received and whose feet were fastened in the stocks in an inner cell. Yet they were singing hymns in praise of the God who would not keep them from all the embarrassment. What a foolish thing to do! But they prayed and sang and continued to do so. The devil could have been laughing at their foolishness. Then suddenly, there came such a violent earthquake that shook the foundations of the prison, flew open the prison doors, and loosened every prisoner's chains. The whole episode culminated in the salvation of the jailer and his household, and the next morning, Paul and Silas were released. The devil meant to clip their wings and stop them from preaching the gospel, but through prayer and praise, the table was turned and the persecution rather enhanced the gospel and saving of souls to his shame and frustration.

Paul was one man who humiliated the devil through his attitude of praise in the face of adversity. He wrote his amazing letter to the Philippian church from prison and in it he displayed a rare and admirable attitude of praise. Rather than bemoan his prison chains, he found reasons to rejoice in it. He perceived his chains as a means of advancing the gospel throughout the palace, among the guards and everyone else. He saw that his chains rather encouraged most of the brothers in the Lord to speak the word of the Lord more courageously and fearlessly. He also repeatedly enjoined the Philippian brethren to rejoice always in the Lord. He emphatically wrote, "Rejoice in the Lord always. I will say it again: Rejoice!" (Phil. 4:4). Such a statement coming from someone in prison is unbelievable, considering that the prison is a place of gloom and hopelessness. This must be very frustrating to the devil, who sought to blur his perception of God.

Indeed, the Scripture is filled with men who praised God amid suffering and persecution. Men like Abraham who strengthened his faith and gave glory to God as he waited for years, even onto old age, for the promised child (Rom. 4: 18-21); and men like the disciples of Jesus who rejoiced that they were counted worthy to suffer disgrace for the name of Jesus after being flogged for the sake of the gospel (Acts 5: 41). Habakkuk summarized such a victorious attitude when he declared:

> [17]Though the fig tree does not bud and there
> are no grapes on the vines, though the olive crop
> fails and the fields produce no food, though

there are no sheep in the pen and no cattle in the stalls,
   <sup>18</sup>yet I will rejoice in the LORD,
   I will be joyful in God my Savior (Hab. 3:17-18).

Horatio G. Spafford was a successful attorney in Chicago and a committed Christian. In 1873, Spafford decided to take his wife and four daughters on a vacation to Europe. He also planned to help out in the Moody-Sankey meeting taking place there.

Owing to an urgent business, Spafford could not travel as scheduled but sent his wife and daughters ahead of him on the ship *S. S. Ville du Harve* and planned to join them soon.

Halfway across the Atlantic, the ship was struck by an English vessel and sank, and all four of Spafford's daughters drowned along with 222 others. Mrs. Spafford was among the few miraculous survivors.

Later, Spafford traveled to rejoin his sorrowing wife in Cardiff. When the ship in which he traveled passed the approximate place where his four daughters drowned, he received such comfort from God he was able to write the words of the hymn, "It is Well with My Soul." The first stanza of the hymn says,

When peace, like a river, attended my soul
When sorrows like sea billow roll—Whatever
my lot, Thou hast made me to say,
It is well, it is well with my soul.

(TanBible.com, "200 Amazing Hymn Stories," prepared by staff, Bible Communications, Inc. http://www.tanbible.com/tol_sng/itiswellwithmysoul.htm.

That is an amazing story of victory through praise.

I also heard the chilling testimony of a famous Nigerian preacher, Rev. Dr. Uma Ukpai. Hear him:

> By 5am that day, armed robbers broke into my office and removed everything here. By 4pm same day, my car plunged into the river with my three children. The driver headed towards a bend and when he applied the brake, the car somersaulted into the river. When I came in to rescue the children, my wife also dived in behind me.
>
> Remember that I grew up in Rivers State as a result of which I can swim. While I was swimming against the current towards the car to rescue the children, a voice said to me that your wife was drowning behind. I left the children and went for her. I carried her with one hand and swam to the shore where I kept her in safety.
>
> I went back to the river for the children because a child stays alive in water for about two and half hours. I rescued them (two children and two cousins) and put them in another car. We had not driven up to five minutes, when an oncoming vehicle ran into us. The impact was such that the bonnet and bumper of our car flew out. I stepped out of the car and was pacing up and down when somebody ran up to me to inform me that the bus being used by my musical group caught fire. (Uma, U. 2006. "Day God refused to hear my prayer," Eternal life Christian Online magazine.

Accessed July 2, 2010, http://www.elifeonline.
net/elife4-jan-2006/interview-uma-ukpai)

He lost his two children in the accident. He still proceeded
to preach at the crusade that night. At the crusade, he sang as
follows:

> *Ma m enweghi ihe enwere m Jisos,*
> *O dighi ihe koro m moli.*

Meaning: If I have nothing but Jesus,
I lack nothing at all.

Those were men who have really touched the heart of God
and frustrated the devil. Great is their reward in heaven (Matt.
5:12).

I recall my joy in my early days in faith each time my
schoolmates made fun of me for my new faith. I recall how
I would exceedingly rejoice and praise God after each such
experience. I would say to myself, Can this be true—people
making fun of me for Christ's sake? Wow! That means my faith
is real. I'm indeed a child of God. I would remember Matthew
5:11-12 and really thank God for truly making me His child.

We may wonder why believers adopt the option of praise in
adverse circumstances. I can think of two reasons:

1. Knowledge of God;
2. Faith in God.

In Daniel 11:32, the Scripture says, "But the people that
do know their God shall be strong and do exploits" (KJV).
Such men having proved God over and over in their daily

walk believe in His power. Drawing from his experience in the field as a shepherd, when face to face with the Philistine giant, Goliath, David said, "The LORD who delivered me from the paw of the lion and the paw of the bear will deliver me from the hand of this Philistine" (1 Sam. 17:37). People who adopt the option of praise in adversity trust in God—His power and might, His word, His love, and His faithfulness. They know that God has power to do anything He wants to do. He has power to have stopped the affliction from coming on them in the first place; and He has the power to stop it at any time. They trust that God means well by allowing it and will work out something good through it for them and for His glory (Rom. 8:28, 1 Thess. 5:18). They trust in His love and thoughts toward them (Rom. 8:35, 38-39; Jer. 29:11). They understand by God's word that the affliction is just a trial of their faith and that it is momentary (Jas. 1:2-3; 1 Pet. 1:6). Consequently, they rejoice and glorify God in it. The attitude of praise in adversity; therefore, is a product of knowledge and faith in God. That attitude extols God above the problem.

> **People who adopt the option of praise in adversity trust in God—His power and might, His word, His love, and His faithfulness.**

How does God feel when His children praise Him in the face of trouble? I believe God is thrilled. He feels proud and moves into action on their behalf. I will never forget what God told us one day in a church service as we worshipped Him through songs. He said, "Learn to praise me. Praise brings my presence, and my presence brings my glory. I dwell in the praises of my people." To me, that was a great eye-opener. See once again the glaring example in 2 Chron. 20:21-22 when King Jehoshaphat's army began to sing in the face of the invading armies: "As they began to sing and praise, the Lord sent ambushes against the men of Ammon and Moab and Mount Seir who were invading Judah and they were defeated." Notice that the Lord acted in response to their praise. God inhabits the praises of His people (Ps. 22:3). See again the example of Paul and Silas in prison (Acts 16: 25-26): "About midnight Paul and Silas were praying and singing hymns to God, and the other prisoners were listening to them. Suddenly there was such a violent earthquake that the foundations of the prison were shaken. At once all the prison doors flew open, and everybody's chains came loose." Again notice that God acted in response to their prayer and hymns of praise. It's fantastic.

We should, however, note that God doesn't always intervene immediately in response to praise. Certainly, in all cases of sincere praise to God, He is proud of His child who praises in suffering. Nevertheless, there are times He will sovereignly allow the situation to linger despite praises. In such a situation, He gives more grace to the believer to endure the suffering. That was true in Job's case. Despite the fact that Job praised God after losing all his possessions, God still allowed Satan to continue bombarding Job, but made His grace sufficient for him to go through it all blameless. Through all this, Job did not sin against God by speaking ill of Him. At last, God made him prosperous again and gave him twice as much as he had previously. He made his latter part greater than his first and also blessed him with long life so that he saw his children and their children to the fourth generation (Job 42:7,10-17). When He allows adversity to persist despite praise, He wants to work out His glory in His own special way. At the end, He blesses His child who has honored Him in that circumstance.

Praise in the midst of adversity is a sign of maturity in the Lord. It is a veritable weapon that frustrates and devastates the devil, gives victory to the believer, and brings glory to God. In 1 Thess. 5:18, the Scripture says, "In everything give thanks for this is God's will for you in Christ Jesus." Those who live by this injunction gain great victories because they thank God and praise Him both when their situation is good and when it is bad. They trust that God works in all things for their good (Rom. 8:28). God is proud of such children and manifests Himself on their behalf.

> **Praise in the midst of adversity is a sign of maturity in the Lord. It is a veritable weapon that frustrates and devastates the devil, gives victory to the believer, and brings glory to God.**

# Chapter Seven

## God Knows When and How to Announce a Man

While in my office one morning in 2007, God dropped these words in my heart: "God knows when and how to announce a man." He referred me to the anointing of David as king of Israel. Permit me to share the message I received that morning. In 1 Samuel 16: 1-13 we read:

> ¹The LORD said to Samuel, "How long will you mourn for Saul, since I have rejected him as king over Israel? Fill your horn with oil and be on your way; I am sending you to Jesse of Bethlehem. I have chosen one of his sons to be king."
> ²But Samuel said, "How can I go? Saul will hear about it and kill me."
> The LORD said, "Take a heifer with you and say, 'I have come to sacrifice to the LORD.'
> ³Invite Jesse to the sacrifice, and I will show you what to do. You are to anoint for me the one I indicate."

⁴Samuel did what the LORD said. When he arrived at Bethlehem, the elders of the town trembled when they met him. They asked, "Do you come in peace?"

⁵Samuel replied, "Yes, in peace; I have come to sacrifice to the LORD. Consecrate yourselves and come to the sacrifice with me." Then he consecrated Jesse and his sons and invited them to the sacrifice.

⁶When they arrived, Samuel saw Eliab and thought, "Surely the LORD's anointed stands here before the LORD."

⁷But the LORD said to Samuel, "Do not consider his appearance or his height, for I have rejected him. The LORD does not look at the things man looks at. Man looks at the outward appearance, but the LORD looks at the heart."

⁸Then Jesse called Abinadab and had him pass in front of Samuel. But Samuel said, "The LORD has not chosen this one either." ⁹ Jesse then had Shammah pass by, but Samuel said, "Nor has the LORD chosen this one."

¹⁰Jesse had seven of his sons pass before Samuel, but Samuel said to him, "The LORD has not chosen these."

¹¹So he asked Jesse, "Are these all the sons you have?"

"There is still the youngest," Jesse answered, "but he is tending the sheep."

Samuel said, "Send for him; we will not sit down until he arrives."

¹²So he sent and had him brought in. He was ruddy, with a fine appearance and handsome features.

Then the LORD said, "Rise and anoint him; he is the one."

¹³So Samuel took the horn of oil and anointed him in the presence of his brothers, and from that day on the Spirit of the LORD came upon David in power. Samuel then went to Ramah.

God had chosen the little boy David to be the next king of Israel, but nobody knew it. The boy David was a shepherd and tended his father's sheep. He was the youngest of his father's eight sons. God chose when and how to announce His choice of David to his father's family. He sent the prophet, Samuel, to anoint him as king as seen in the above account. Notice how his father presented his seven sons he believed God could choose from. He did not think David fit for consideration, probably, because he was still a boy. He did not know what was in him. Notice also how even the prophet, Samuel, was deceived by the physical appearance of Eliab, and he thought, "Surely, the LORD's anointed stands here before the LORD" (v.6). Save for God's intervention, Samuel would have gone ahead to anoint him. God rejected all the seven sons that Jesse presented.

Samuel then asked Jesse, "Are these all the sons you have?" (v.11). It was only then that Jesse mentioned David. Just listen to Samuel's response, "Send for him; we will not sit down until he arrives" (v.11). He sent for him. As he arrived, the Lord said to Samuel, "Rise and anoint him; he is the one" (v.12). Samuel took the horn of oil, anointed David in the presence of his brothers, and from that day on the Spirit of the Lord came upon David in power. Awesome!

It tells me that when God's time to manifest a man comes, nothing can stop Him, for His plan cannot be thwarted (Job 42:2). He will fish the man out from wherever he is and manifest him His way. Even if the man is tucked away in a wilderness like David or in a dungeon like Joseph, He will bring him out to take possession of his inheritance.

It also tells me that it is not what man thinks but what God thinks that prevails. David's father did not give him a chance at all in his heart. Hence, he did not bother to present him for consideration. Samuel himself would have given the position to another man judging by outward appearance. But none of those prevailed. To establish God's choice, Samuel was compelled to command: "Send for him; we will not sit down until he arrives." They had to mount a guard of honor for David as he arrived. When God's time comes for your manifestation, every opposition against you will mount a guard of honor for you, by force. Every opposition stands still for you. It is what God says about you that prevails, not what any man says or thinks. Notice the sense of urgency in Samuel's command. It is reminiscent of that shown in pharaoh's command to fetch Joseph from the dungeon when it was time for his manifestation (Gen. 41:14). When it is God's time to announce a man, He attaches some urgency to it, and everything and everybody must cooperate to facilitate the announcement.

> **When God's time comes for your manifestation, every opposition against you will mount a guard of honor for you, by force.**

Again, note that the anointing was done "in the presence of his brothers." This was to make God's choice and election clear to every member of the family for avoidance of doubt. When

God decides to manifest a man, He makes it abundantly clear to everyone concerned.

**When it is God's time to announce a man, He attaches some urgency to it, and everything and everybody must cooperate to facilitate the announcement.**

In explaining these things to me, He related the story to my life. God had promised me great blessings, among which was taking me to reside in the United States of America. As time went on, however, nothing seemed to work out for me, and there were no signs of those promises coming to pass. On my own, I made several efforts with the help of my brothers to travel to the United States, but to no avail. Neither was I able to get a truly good job as a consolation, after several years of joblessness. After a time, I got a job that I thought could be close to what I expected but, alas, it was not as I thought. Worse still, I was posted away from the state capital where I lived to a sub-urban community, which resulted in my living separately from my family—something I never desired. While there, I put my best into the job, but nobody seemed to notice my efforts. I was getting frustrated, but I kept drawing encouragement from the word of God. Everything looked gloomy, and I felt lost in that community. Then one day, the word of God I now share came to me while I was sitting in my office: "God knows when and how to announce a man." Those words ministered great encouragement and hope to me. It was like God saying to me, "Relax, I know when and how to bring to pass all my promises to you." I relaxed. Soon after, God began to fulfill His promises. First, I was re-posted back to Enugu, the state capital, and I rejoined my family. Secondly, in the same month I arrived back to the city, God gave me a new job as the managing director of a microfinance bank, a very important position. God completely worked out the job offer by Himself. I did not know about the job opening; neither did I apply for it. I simply received a voice message and a text message on my phone, both asking me to call a certain number for an important discussion. I called the number and behold, it was the chairman of the bank, and he invited me to a meeting with him in his office. Eventually, after due process, I got the job. It was a good job with great prospects, but God was not done yet. Thirdly, after a few months on the job, He confirmed me a winner of the United States diversity visa lottery. After exactly one year on the job, God flew me and my family on eagle's wings to the United States, where we live today as permanent residents. Thus, God made it clear it was time to announce his servant and people who watched the sequence of upliftments marveled and glorified God.

**When God decides to manifest a man, He makes it abundantly clear to everyone concerned.**

The one thing to note is that when God's time comes, He makes the announcement in a way that will make it clear to everybody, including the person involved, that it is His doing so that the glory will be His. God fulfilled His promise of taking me to the United States of America exactly twenty-one years after He gave me the promise. This is very similar to Joseph's case. God had shown him he was going to be a ruler, but it took several years including being sold into slavery before He made him a ruler. From the time he was sold into slavery to when he became a ruler, thirteen years passed. At the appointed time, however, God made good on His promise. To Him, time is not a problem. With the Lord, a thousand years are like a day (2 Pet. 3:8). In its time, He makes everything beautiful (Ecc. 3:11). How I played the visa lottery is another testimony by itself, as I did not believe in it. But suffice it to say that God simply imposed it on me, and I still marvel at that. God is able to impose His blessing on a man He has decided to favor. He continued the announcement in the United States. He speedily fitted my family into the system by providing jobs for me and my wife despite the recession in the country. And, in just over one year, He blessed us with an exquisitely beautiful house of our own—a house many have simply described as a mansion. Thus, God enabled us to perform a rare feat that left people amazed.

In Isaiah 55:8-9 the Scripture says,
8"For my thoughts are not your thoughts, neither are your ways my ways," declares the LORD.
9"As the heavens are higher than the earth, so are my ways higher than your ways and my thoughts than your thoughts.

This is so true. We usually have our ways and thoughts about how things will work out and they are, most of the time, different from God's. He is sovereign and has planned out our lives quite in advance. He has an appointed time for everything and knows how to work out every aspect of our lives once the time comes. For us, any time is right, but for God, there is the right time (Jn. 7:6, 8). He says:

1There is a time for everything, and a season for every activity under heaven:
2a time to be born and a time to die, a time to plant and a time to uproot,

³a time to kill and a time to heal, a time to tear down and a time to build,

⁴a time to weep and a time to laugh, a time to mourn and a time to dance,

⁵a time to scatter stones and a time to gather them, a time to embrace and a time to refrain,

⁶a time to search and a time to give up, a time to keep and a time to throw away,

⁷a time to tear and a time to mend, a time to be silent and a time to speak,

⁸a time to love and a time to hate, a time for war and a time for peace (Eccl. 3:1-8).

**For us, any time is right, but for God, there is the right time (Jn. 7:6, 8).**

He is a God of order. In Acts 1:6 Jesus's disciples wanted to know if it was time for Him to restore the kingdom to Israel. But Jesus answered them instructively, saying, "It is not for you to know the times and dates the Father has set by his own authority" (Acts 1:7). This is what He still tells us concerning His promises to us. It is not for us to know the times and dates the Father has set by His own authority. Ours is to trust and follow Him. The Scripture admonishes us to imitate those who through faith and patience inherit what has been promised (Heb. 6:12). It takes faith and patience to obtain the fulfillment of God's promises in our lives. Has God given you a vision or a promise? It is for an appointed time. Though it tarries, wait for it, it will not delay (Hab. 2:3). At the fullness of time, the faithful God will bring it to pass. It will not delay by a second.

You know what? You can't hurry God because he knows what He is doing. You've got to wait for Him, for He will certainly come right on time. I recall how, in the years of my waiting, I always cried to God to quickly come to my rescue, but each time He would say, "Wait!" After a while I got tired of hearing, "Wait!" and each time I finished agonizing in His presence, I would jump out to avoid hearing it. Yet I couldn't push Him to hurry. He continued coming slowly but steadily. God is majestic and walks majestically—never in a hurry until His time comes. He knows He is always in control. I am still waiting for the fulfillment of a lot more of His promises to me, but I have learned my lessons. Sometimes, we want Him to do it quickly to prove a point—for instance, to vindicate us as His children, or so that doubters will believe, or for His own glory, etc. God knows all those things and knows how to work out His glory. He is God. We cannot persuade Him to come quickly contrary to His will. He knows the end from the beginning. We are short-sighted, but He sees the big picture.

> **God is majestic and walks majestically—never in a hurry until His time comes.**

Where has God placed you now? A place where there seems to be no sign of light in sight? All you need to do is to be faithful in service there. Serve faithfully, patiently, and heartily. He is watching and taking note of your faithfulness and sacrifices. Man may forget you, but He can't. Listen to what He says to you:

> [15]"Can a mother forget the baby at her breast
> and have no compassion on the child she has borne?
> Though she may forget,
> I will not forget you!

<sup>16</sup> See, I have engraved you on the palms of my hands; your walls are ever before me (Is. 49:15-16).

He has engraved you on the palms of His hands so that He will not forget. He is also crediting your faithfulness and patience to you. At His appointed time, He will fish you out and publicly announce you. That was what he did for David and Joseph. David was faithful as a shepherd. Joseph was patient and faithful as a slave in Egypt. At the fullness of time, God retrieved them and announced them. He has not changed. He is still the same and will do the same for you if you believe. He knows exactly when and how to do it in your own case.

# Chapter Eight

## Your Heavenly Father Knows You Have Need of These Things

As he traveled deeper into the interior, many hardships befell him. The slave-traders had burned hundreds of villages and it was almost impossible to obtain food. "I took up my belt three holes to relieve hunger," he wrote in his journal. Worst of all, one of his men ran off with his precious medicine box. Now he had no quinine with which to fight the ever recurring fever. "This loss," he says, "is like the sentence of death." Ill with fever and half-starved, he staggered along . . . . All his companions deserted him but three. Finally he reached Ujiji, only "a ruckle of bones," to find that all his provisions and goods had been stolen. He felt himself to be the man who was robbed and left helpless on the Jericho Road, but he did not know that the Good Samaritan was close at hand.

One of his men rushed up shouting, "A white man is coming! Look!" Down the village path walked a white man at the head of a caravan of African followers with the flag of the United States unfurled over their heads. It was Henry M. Stanley, happy to find Livingstone at last. Livingstone was very happy, too. This was the first white man he had seen in five years. Moreover, Stanley brought a quantity of wholesome food for him and letters from his children in England.

"How do you come to be in this remote place?" inquired Livingstone. Then Stanley told how, exactly two years before, he had been summoned by James Gordon Bennett of the New York Herald, who said: "Stanley, it is reported that David Livingstone is dead. I do not believe it. He is far away in Central Africa, lost, ill and stranded. I want you to go and find Livingstone, and give him any help he needs. Never mind the cost. Go and find Livingstone, and bring him back to the civilized world." (Harrison 1954)

That was the story of David Livingstone, the missionary and pathfinder of Africa. God had known that someday he would be in that desperate state and, two years earlier, orchestrated the sending of Henry Stanley to Central Africa to look for him. I can imagine how Stanley might have wandered about the entire region of the continent all the time, looking for him. Can you imagine the miraculous "coincidence" of their paths meeting in the nick of time? It shows how much God cares for His children, especially when we walk in His will. He sees and plans for our tomorrow. This reminds me of how God planned ahead of time for Jacob and his family in regard to a future famine that would ravage the entire world. He allowed Joseph to be sold twenty years ahead of time as a slave to Egypt. Nobody knew that God was simply sending him ahead to preserve his father's family from starving to death in a future devastating famine. God made Joseph a ruler over Egypt thirteen years after he arrived in the country as a slave. His first seven years in power saw food surplus in the land. This was followed by a seven years of severe famine, but by divine wisdom Joseph had stored up enough food from the surpluses of the preceding years to sustain the people of the land and, indeed, most of the world, for another seven years. Consequently, all Egypt and the other countries in the region depended on Joseph for provision. God's purpose in all this was revealed when Joseph's father, Jacob, and his family, including his brothers who sold him into slavery, moved to Egypt following the famine, at Joseph's invitation. In Egypt, they were amply provided for by Joseph and that way they were preserved. After the death of Jacob, Joseph's brothers, fearing that Joseph might pay them back in their own coin, went to him to ask for forgiveness. Joseph, once again, shared with them his understanding of the purpose of God in all this. He said to his brothers, "Don't be afraid. Am I in the place of God? You intended to harm me, but God intended it for good to accomplish what is now being done, the saving of many lives. 21 So then, don't be afraid. I will provide for you and your children . . ." (Gen. 50: 19-21). And with those words, he reassured them of his continuing kindness. Joseph understood that God allowed all that happened to him for the purpose of preserving his life and those of his father's family during the famine. God plans ahead for His children. You may not see it, but God is always working behind the scene for your provision.

When we walk in His will, He provides for us. He knows our needs. I see something that God does in Genesis 22. God tested Abraham by asking him to offer his only son, Isaac, as a burnt offering to Him on a mountain in Moriah. Having given the instruction to Abraham, God went ahead of him to the mountain and waited for him with a ram for the sacrifice. It took Abraham obeying God to realize that God had made a provision for the offering instead of his son. Had he offered his son anywhere else, he would not have realized the provision God had made for him. When Abraham saw the ram God had provided on the mountain, he took it and sacrificed it as a burnt offering instead of his son in keeping with God's bidding. Thereafter, he called that place "Jehovahjireh" meaning, "The Lord will provide." And, arising from that, to this day, it is said, "On the mountain of the Lord it will be provided." Note that it is "on the mountain of the Lord," not anywhere else, that it will be provided. That means that God provides for us when we are where He wants us to be and doing what He wants us to do—when we are in His will. Inside His will is provision for our sustenance, and only those who walk in obedience access the provision. Outside His will, there is no guarantee of His provision. David confirmed this when he said, "I was young and now I am old, yet I have never seen the righteous forsaken or their children begging bread," (Ps. 37:25). Why? The Lord surely provides for them. God is faithful in providing for the righteous. The righteous is one who walks in obedience to God.

---

**You may not see it, but God is always working behind the scene for your provision.**

---

In Matthew 6:25-34, Jesus taught His disciples, saying:

> [25]"Therefore I tell you, do not worry about your life, what you will eat or drink; or about your body, what you will wear. Is not life more

important than food, and the body more important than clothes?

> **Inside His will is provision for our sustenance, and only those who walk in obedience access the provision. Outside His will, there is no guarantee of His provision.**

²⁶Look at the birds of the air; they do not sow or reap or store away in barns, and yet your heavenly Father feeds them. Are you not much more valuable than they?

²⁷Who of you by worrying can add a single hour to his life?

²⁸"And why do you worry about clothes? See how the lilies of the field grow. They do not labor or spin.

²⁹Yet I tell you that not even Solomon in his entire splendor was dressed like one of these.

³⁰If that is how God clothes the grass of the field, which is here today and tomorrow is thrown into the fire, will he not much more clothe you, O you of little faith?

³¹So do not worry, saying, 'What shall we eat?' or 'What shall we drink?' or 'What shall we wear?'

³²For the pagans run after all these things and your heavenly Father knows that you need them.

³³But seek first his kingdom and his righteousness, and all these things will be given to you as well.

<sup>34</sup>Therefore do not worry about tomorrow, for tomorrow will worry about itself. Each day has enough trouble of its own.

Let's look at what Jesus is saying here. He wants us to have understanding. He says we should not worry about our lives and our bodies—what we will eat or drink and what we will wear. Food is for life and clothes for the body. He asks, "Is not life more important than food, and the body more important than clothes?" If God has made the more important life, will He not provide the less important food to sustain it? And if He has made the more important body, will He not provide the less important clothes to cover the body? If He is able to do the bigger thing, is He not able to do the smaller thing? If He is able to create the important thing, is He not responsible enough to take care of it? He drives the point home with an interesting analogy. He calls our attention to the birds of the air and the grass of the field. He reminds us that the birds of the air neither sow nor reap nor store away in barns. That means they own nothing. Yet they don't starve. Why? Our heavenly Father feeds them? How? I don't know, but He does. He then asks, "Are you not more valuable than they?" He is saying, "If God cares so much for the less valuable birds of the air, will He not much more care for the more valuable you?" It follows that He will feed us much more than He feeds these birds. He is getting us to think and understand. He asks, "Who of you by worrying can add a single hour to his life? That means, "Left alone, who of you can extend this life you are so concerned about by one single hour just by worrying?" Nobody, of course. He wants us to see the folly of worrying. Again, He reminds us of the lilies of the field, how they grow and are clothed, even though they neither labor nor spin. Who nurtures and clothes them? God. The grass of the field has such brief life and value that today it is here and tomorrow is cast into fire. Yet God cares about it and beautifully clothes it. He is saying, "If God so clothes the 'worthless' grass of the field, will He not much more clothe us—those who bear His image?"

Jesus therefore identifies our problem as little faith. That means, not believing in God enough. Our problem is that we sometimes equate ourselves with God without knowing it. We think that His infinite wisdom and power are like ours, and when we are overwhelmed by something or cannot figure something out, we think He has the same problem. That way, we bring the infinite God to our finite level and we worry, not knowing what to do. Jesus appears to be lamenting when He says, "O you of little faith." Then He admonishes us not to worry about what to eat, what to drink, or what to wear saying, "For . . . your heavenly Father knows that you need them." He is summarily saying, "If He knows that the birds of the air and the grass of the field need these things and provides them with those, He also knows you have need of them and will much more provide them for you." He then tells us what to do: "But seek first his kingdom and his righteousness, and all these things will be given to you as well." God wants us to seek Him, seek His Lordship, and obey Him, period. He promises that we will find His kingdom and righteousness, and He will additionally give us these things—supply our needs. Food, drink, and clothes represent all our needs—whatever they are. He says the pagans (people who don't know God) run after all these things but that we, His children, should not, because our heavenly Father knows we need them and will provide them for us, duly. He says we should not worry about tomorrow because tomorrow will worry about itself. He wants us to take life one day at a time and cast all our cares on God because He cares for us (1 Pet. 5:7). This is how God wants us to live.

> **Our problem is that we sometimes equate ourselves with God without knowing it. We think that His infinite wisdom and power are like ours, and when we are overwhelmed by something or cannot figure something out, we think He has the same problem. That way, we bring the infinite God to our finite level and we worry, not knowing what to do.**

Obedience is the key to God's provision. Jesus's mother gave us this key at the wedding that took place at Canaan in Galilee to which Jesus and His disciples were invited (Jn. 2: 1-11). When the wine for the feast was exhausted, Jesus's mother approached Him for help, but Jesus told her that His time had not yet come. Nevertheless, His mother said to the servants, "Do whatever he tells you." Therein lies the key—obedience. The need of the hour was provision, and Mary gave the servants the key: "Do whatever he tells you." Mary, being His mother, knew her Son and how to win His heart. Therefore, she told the servants precisely what to do—obey Him. Jesus told the servants to fill the six water jars nearby with water. He did not tell them why, and neither did they ask him. They obeyed and filled them with water. Then he told them to draw some out and take it to the master of the feast. Again, they obeyed, and the water turned into sweeter wine than the one earlier served. You see, through obedience, the need of the occasion was met.

> **Obedience is the key to God's provision.**

Peter and some of the disciples once learned a hard lesson on not walking in obedience—trying to provide for themselves by themselves. Let's look at the account in John 21:1-14:

¹Afterward Jesus appeared again to his disciples, by the Sea of Tiberias. It happened this way:

²Simon Peter, Thomas (called Didymus), Nathanael from Cana in Galilee, the sons of Zebedee, and two other disciples were together.

³"I'm going out to fish," Simon Peter told them, and they said, "We'll go with you." So they went out and got into the boat, but that night they caught nothing.

⁴Early in the morning, Jesus stood on the shore, but the disciples did not realize that it was Jesus.

⁵He called out to them, "Friends, haven't you any fish?"

"No," they answered.

⁶He said, "Throw your net on the right side of the boat and you will find some." When they did, they were unable to haul the net in because of the large number of fish.

⁷Then the disciple whom Jesus loved said to Peter, "It is the Lord!" As soon as Simon Peter heard him say, "It is the Lord," he wrapped his outer garment around him (for he had taken it off) and jumped into the water.

⁸The other disciples followed in the boat, towing the net full of fish, for they were not far from shore, about a hundred yards.

⁹When they landed, they saw a fire of burning coals there with fish on it, and some bread.

¹⁰Jesus said to them, "Bring some of the fish you have just caught."

¹¹Simon Peter climbed aboard and dragged the net ashore. It was full of large fish, 153, but even with so many the net was not torn.

¹²Jesus said to them, "Come and have breakfast." None of the disciples dared ask him, "Who are you?" They knew it was the Lord.

¹³Jesus came, took the bread and gave it to them, and did the same with the fish.

¹⁴This was now the third time Jesus appeared to his disciples after he was raised from the dead.

Recall that Peter and some of the disciples, including Andrew, James, and John, were professional fishermen before Jesus called them to follow Him. Here is a recap of how they were called:

¹One day as Jesus was standing by the Lake of Gennesaret, with the people crowding around him and listening to the word of God,

²he saw at the water's edge two boats, left there by the fishermen, who were washing their nets.

³He got into one of the boats, the one belonging to Simon, and asked him to put out a little from shore. Then he sat down and taught the people from the boat.

⁴When he had finished speaking, he said to Simon, "Put out into deep water, and let down the nets for a catch."

⁵Simon answered, "Master, we've worked hard all night and haven't caught anything. But because you say so, I will let down the nets."

⁶When they had done so, they caught such a large number of fish that their nets began to break.

⁷So they signaled their partners in the other boat to come and help them, and they came and filled both boats so full that they began to sink.

⁸When Simon Peter saw this, he fell at Jesus's knees and said, "Go away from me, Lord; I am a sinful man!"

⁹For he and all his companions were astonished at the catch of fish they had taken,

¹⁰and so were James and John, the sons of Zebedee, Simon's partners.

Then Jesus said to Simon, "Don't be afraid; from now on you will catch men."

¹¹So they pulled their boats up on shore, left everything and followed him (Lk. 5: 1-11).

Following the astonishing catch of a large number of fish at Jesus's word in that first meeting with Him, they quickly responded to Jesus's invitation. They left everything, including the staggering number of fish and their boats, and followed Him. They trusted that if He could do such a thing in one swoop, He would be able to provide for them at all times. They trusted in His ability to provide for them. From then on, they ceased to be fishermen and joined Jesus in fishing men. Of course, as long as they trusted and walked with Jesus, He never failed to provide for them.

After the death of Jesus, however, Peter obviously began to entertain some doubt about Jesus's ability to provide for them despite the fact that He had risen from the dead. He was relapsing into the problem Jesus had identified and lamented about in Matthew 6:30: little faith. He felt he should start helping himself. He remembered his profession, his skills, and expertise in it. One day, he told the other disciples, "I'm going out to fish." And behold, they were all having the same problem. So they replied, "We'll go with you." Not even one person objected. How fickle we can sometimes be. It also shows the awesome influence of leadership. It shows how influential Peter was as the leader of the disciples. This calls for caution on the path of every leader. They all went out to the sea and got into the boat and began fishing. But they toiled all night and caught nothing. They exhausted their skills and expertise but caught nothing. Because they were walking in disobedience, without God on their side, they toiled in vain. This reminds me of the word of God in Psalm 127: 1-2: "Unless the LORD builds the house, its builders labor in vain . . . . In vain you rise early and stay up late, toiling for food to eat . . . ."

Early in the morning, Jesus appeared on the shore, but they did not recognize him. He said to them, "Friends, haven't you any fish?" "No," they answered. Jesus was really asking, "Friends, can I see the fish you have caught by your own efforts?" And their answer was "None." None, because they worked alone—they were on their own. Then He decided to show them the difference. He said to them, "Throw your net on the right side of the boat and you will find some." They did, and they were unable to haul in the net because of the large number of fish they caught. Wow! What a difference it makes to be guided by the word of God. It is God that makes the difference. As all knowing, He knows exactly where the fish are. When we walk without Him, we toil blindly and depend on chance for success. We dissipate a lot of energy and time, unnecessarily, with nothing to show for it. But when we are guided by God, we hit right on target. We save energy and time, and yet with high productivity; we do the right thing at the right time, and we see success. The truth is: left alone, we cannot provide for ourselves. Jesus says, "Apart from me you can do nothing" (Jn. 15:5). Absolutely nothing!

Immediately, John exclaimed, "It is the Lord!" I suppose the astounding catch quickly reminded him of their first encounter with Jesus. He realized it's only Him who could do this, and his eyes were opened to see it was the Lord. They quickly dragged the fish ashore. On the shore, they saw a fire of burning coals with fish on it and some bread. Jesus then invited them to come and have breakfast. He took the fish and bread and gave to them and they ate. Notice that they came up the shore to meet some fish on fire for them, provided, not by themselves, but by Jesus. The very thing they went toiling for in disobedience was there waiting for them free of charge. More than that, there was also some bread with it. So Jesus had for them more than they were looking for. Had they remained in obedience, they would have spared themselves the trouble of expending energy fishing as well as denying themselves of a good night's sleep. Yet they would have enjoyed more than they expected—fish and bread instead of just fish. God is so loving and caring, but we don't know it. He is such a responsible Father, but we underestimate His love, power, and sense of responsibility. I'm sure it grieves Him. That is why He laments, "My people are destroyed for lack of knowledge" (Hos. 4:6). He means our lack of knowledge of His power, love, word, character, and faithfulness. Because of the problem of ignorance, God's children are caught up in the rat race of our time. They run helter-skelter, chasing after the very things the Lord says the pagans run after—the very things He says will be added to them. They reverse the order He has set for them. They want to seek first what to eat, what to drink, and what to wear, hoping, afterwards, to seek His kingdom and His righteousness. They put the cart before the horse. They work round the clock, pursuing these things. Consequently, they have no time for the work of the Lord, and His work suffers. They thereby deny Him the opportunity to vindicate His word. Most of us are guilty of this. We rely on human wisdom—common sense—rather than the word of God. I believe He is earnestly looking for those who will trust and obey Him in this matter so He can prove His faithfulness to them. He wants to take the heat off us and make things easier for us. He wants to think for us, but we choose to think for ourselves.

> **When we walk without Him, we toil blindly and depend on chance for success. We dissipate a lot of energy and time, unnecessarily, with nothing to show for it. But when we are guided by God, we hit right on target. We save energy and time, and yet with high productivity; we do the right thing at the right time, and we see success. The truth is: left alone, we cannot provide for ourselves. Jesus says, "Apart from me you can do nothing" (Jn. 15:5). Absolutely nothing!**

When my family got the opportunity to emigrate to the United States of America, we had two challenges: 1.) How to raise enough money to execute the movement; and 2.) How to be sustained in the US, considering the serious economic recession then in the country. Both needs bordered on provision. As we sought the Lord concerning the first challenge, He promised to sponsor the project and asked us not to worry about it. The amount required was huge. God went ahead to provide the money and even more. We not only had enough funds to complete the entire project but also had significant surplus to travel with. We did not borrow a dime from anybody. God kept His promise. How He provided the money still amazes us today.

> **Because of the problem of ignorance, God's children are caught up in the rat race of our time. They run helter-skelter, chasing after the very things the Lord says the pagans run after—the very things He says will be added to them.**

For the second challenge, we hatched a plan. We decided that I should take my family to the US and come back to keep my job until my wife, who is a registered nurse, passed her RN board exam and secured a job. The idea was for me to continue supporting my family from Nigeria until my wife got a good job as a nurse. We agreed that thereafter, I would resign my job and join them in the US. The plan made sense to us, but the Lord did not approve of it. He said to me: "Leave everything and follow me. Don't look back." He wanted me to leave everything like His first disciples did and follow Him. He described my plan to go back to Nigeria as looking back. It was a difficult demand considering that I had a good job from which I could support my family. Nevertheless, I obeyed. I left everything and followed Him—a bold step of faith. We did not know that God had perfected arrangements for our sustenance in US before He formed us. Shortly after our arrival in the country, my wife passed her board exam. And soon she got a job, and that was it. We took off immediately from there despite the recession.

You see, before I met Ifeoma, God had known we were going to be married. He had also known that a time would come when our family would move to the United States. He knew that the country would be in recession at the time, so he trained her as a nurse ahead of time. He knew that nursing is one sure and easy way of breaking into the economy at such a time when people were losing their jobs. Soon after, He also provided a job for me. Thus, God fitted us into the economy and ever since He has continued to sustain us, blessing us, as a friend described it, "in leaps and bounds." In just over one year, He blessed us with a big and magnificent house of our own in California. It only took our obedience. God is a perfect planner and meticulous to the core. He makes no mistakes of calculation, omission, or commission. He never says, "Oops!" That word is only for humans.

A Christian friend of mine shared how he found himself in a tight financial corner at a time. He had no money and no job and was squatting with a friend who provided for him. It happened that his friend was out of the country, and he was completely broke. One day, he drove to an office to inquire about job opening and met a lady in the office who told him there was none. He left the office. On entering his car to drive off, he saw the same lady running up to him. She got to him and handed some money, forty dollars, to him. My friend asked what that was for and the lady just said, "I think you might need it." She turned and left. To my friend, it was like manna from heaven. God did that to remind him He was mindful of him. That provision strengthened his faith. Of course, God continued from there until, he was completely sorted out. He never forgets us. He has engraved us on the palms of His hands so as not to forget us (Is. 49:16). More so, He is not a man that can forget.

> **God is a perfect planner and meticulous to the core. He makes no mistakes of calculation, omission, or commission. He never says, "Oops!" That word is only for humans.**

Talking about His ability to provide for all who look up to Him, see what the Scripture says,

²⁴How many are your works, O LORD!

> In wisdom you made them all; the earth is full of your creatures.
> ²⁵There is the sea, vast and spacious, teeming with creatures beyond number—living things both large and small.
> ²⁶There the ships go to and fro, and the leviathan, which you formed to frolic there.
> ²⁷These all look to you to give them their food at the proper time.
> ²⁸When you give it to them, they gather it up; when you open your hand, they are satisfied with good things (Psalm 104:24-28).

He is awesome and is able to provide for all just by opening His hand. More so, He is the creator who created the heavens and the earth and everything in them out of nothing. He calls the things that are not as though they were (Rom. 4: 17). He is more than able to provide for all.

Some may wonder why God allows us to go really hungry sometimes before He does something. I believe He wants to prove us and teach us dependence on Him. Sometimes, He allows us to exhaust our self-sufficiency so that He will become our sufficiency—so that we will learn that the arm of the flesh cannot save. Also, like in every other trial, He allows it in order that our faith, which is of greater value than gold, may be proved genuine and result in praise, glory, and honor when Jesus Christ is revealed (1 Pet. 1:6-7).

Beloved, it is not that God is unwilling or unable to provide for His people; it is that His people do not trust Him enough to provide for them. Consequently, they fail to obey Him and allow Him to provide for them His way. Of course, part of our problem is greed—insatiability. All this is the devil's plan to distract and waste us away. God is always faithful.

# Chapter Nine

## Be Doers Also

Nothing is as important to God as obedience—doing what He says. Samuel said to King Saul, "Does the LORD delight in burnt offerings and sacrifices as much as in obeying the voice of the LORD ? To obey is better than sacrifice, and to heed is better than the fat of rams" (1 Samuel 15:22). The wise man, King Solomon, said, "Now all has been heard; here is the conclusion of the matter: Fear God and keep his commandments, for this is the whole duty of man" (Eccl. 12:13). To fear God is to obey His commands. Fear of God and obedience to Him are inseparable. One cannot claim to fear God if he does not obey Him. The fear of God manifests in obedience to Him. The way we know that a man fears God is when we see how he obeys Him. On the contrary, we say a man does not fear God when he lives without regard to God; when he does what he likes, not minding how God or anybody else feels. That reminds me of what Abraham did in Gerar where he stayed for a while (Gen. 20:1-17). He claimed that Sarah, his beautiful wife, was his sister and asked Sarah to do same in order not to be killed for Sarah's sake. Consequently, the king of the land, Abimelech, sent for Sarah and took her. However, God intervened and warned the king in a dream to return the woman to Abraham because she was his wife. When Abimelech confronted Abraham for lying about Sarah, he replied, "I said to myself, 'There is surely no fear of God in this place, and they will kill me because of my wife'" (v. 11). The implication of his answer is that where there is no fear of God, people do whatever, no matter how bad; they can kill a stranger and take over his wife if they find her attractive. You see, fear of God makes people do right. Fear of God keeps one from sin—disobedience (Exod. 20:20). The way to show God that you fear Him is to obey Him. When God tested Abraham by asking him to sacrifice his only son, Isaac, to Him as a burnt offering, Abraham obeyed. The test was to prove his fear of God. Following his obedience, God said to him, "Now I know that you fear God, because you have not withheld from me your son, your only son" (Gen. 22:12). God was really saying to him, "Now I know that you fear God, because you have obeyed me; not because you said so." It is not just your claiming to fear God that convinces Him you do, but your obedience. Abraham's obedience proved his fear of God.

It's the same with love of God. We say a man loves God when we see how he lives—that he lives in obedience to God. The Scripture says, "This is love for God: to obey his commands" (1 Jn. 5: 3). That is a clear biblical definition of love for God. If anyone therefore claims to love God but does not obey His word, he is a liar and a hypocrite.

> **It is not just your claiming to fear God that convinces Him you do, but your obedience.**

Yet again, the same goes for knowledge of God. We know a man who knows God by how he lives. When a man lives in obedience to the word of God, we say he knows God. This is also biblically true. See what the Scripture says:

³We know that we have come to know him if we obey his commands.

⁴The man who says, "I know him," but does not do what he commands is a liar, and the truth is not in him.

⁵But if anyone obeys his word, God's love is truly made complete in him. This is how we know we are in him:

⁶Whoever claims to live in him must walk as Jesus did (1 John 2: 3-6).

Those who obey his commands live in him, and he in them . . . (1 Jn. 3: 24).

The same is also true of faith in God. James says, "Show me your faith without deeds, and I will show you my faith by what I do" (Jas. 2: 18). The way we know that someone really believes in God is when we see him living in obedience to God not just because he claims to. See what the Scripture says about Abraham: "By faith Abraham, when called to go to a place he would later receive as his inheritance, obeyed and went, even though he did not know where he was going" (Heb. 11: 8). His obedience demonstrated his faith.

This is a clear summary of what it means to fear God, know God, love Him, and have faith in Him. In fact, our relationship with God is defined by how much we obey Him.

God does not joke about obedience. No amount of sacrifice or service will impress him if it is not in keeping with His word. To explain this, let us read the following account:

---

**In fact, our relationship with God is defined by how much we obey Him.**

---

¹David conferred with each of his officers, the commanders of thousands and commanders of hundreds.

²He then said to the whole assembly of Israel, "If it seems good to you and if it is the will of the LORD our God, let us send word far and wide to the rest of our brothers throughout the territories of Israel, and also to the priests and Levites who are with them in their towns and pasturelands, to come and join us.

³Let us bring the ark of our God back to us, for we did not inquire of it during the reign of Saul."

⁴The whole assembly agreed to do this, because it seemed right to all the people.

⁵So David assembled all the Israelites, from the Shihor River in Egypt to Lebo Hamath, to bring the ark of God from Kiriath Jearim.

⁶David and all the Israelites with him went to Baalah of Judah (Kiriath Jearim) to bring up from there the ark of God the LORD, who is enthroned between the cherubim—the ark that is called by the Name.

⁷They moved the ark of God from Abinadab's house on a new cart, with Uzzah and Ahio guiding it.

⁸David and all the Israelites were celebrating with all their might before God, with songs and with harps, lyres, tambourines, cymbals and trumpets.

⁹When they came to the threshing floor of Kidon, Uzzah reached out his hand to steady the ark, because the oxen stumbled.

¹⁰The LORD's anger burned against Uzzah, and he struck him down because he had put his hand on the ark. So he died there before God.

¹¹Then David was angry because the LORD's wrath had broken out against Uzzah, and to this day that place is called Perez Uzzah.

¹²David was afraid of God that day and asked, "How can I ever bring the ark of God to me?"

¹³He did not take the ark to be with him in the City of David. Instead, he took it aside to the house of Obed-Edom the Gittite.

¹⁴The ark of God remained with the family of Obed-Edom in his house for three months, and the LORD blessed his household and everything he had (1 Chronicles 13: 1-14).

David, his officers, and the whole assembly of Israel meant well in deciding to bring back the ark of the Lord. It seemed right to them. They meant to do the will of God but did not inquire as to how. With great zeal, they provided a new cart to bear the ark. As they processed, they celebrated with all their might with songs and musical instruments before the Lord. Ordinarily, one would expect that God Himself would feel honored and elated by all these and overlook whatever they did not do right. But He was not impressed at all. Instead, He burnt with anger. His anger was so much that when Uzzah reached out his hand to steady the ark when the oxen that drove the cart stumbled, He struck him dead immediately. David was angry and afraid to take the ark to the City of David. He then took it aside to the house of Obed-Edom.

Of course, David went home and inquired of the Lord what went wrong. He found out what was the problem: the cart was not properly borne. He then prepared to bear it in keeping with the Lord's prescription. See what he did when he finally went for the cart:

>  ¹After David had constructed buildings for himself in the City of David, he prepared a place for the ark of God and pitched a tent for it.
>
> ²Then David said, "No one but the Levites may carry the ark of God, because the LORD chose them to carry the ark of the LORD and to minister before him forever."
>
> ³David assembled all Israel in Jerusalem to bring up the ark of the LORD to the place he had prepared for it.
>
> ⁴He called together the descendants of Aaron and the Levites . . . .
>
> ¹¹Then David summoned Zadok and Abiathar the priests, and Uriel, Asaiah, Joel, Shemaiah, Eliel and Amminadab the Levites.
>
> ¹²He said to them, "You are the heads of the Levitical families; you and your fellow Levites are to consecrate yourselves and bring up the ark of the LORD, the God of Israel, to the place I have prepared for it.
>
> ¹³It was because you, the Levites, did not bring it up the first time that the LORD our God broke out in anger against us. We did not inquire of him about how to do it in the prescribed way."
>
> ¹⁴So the priests and Levites consecrated themselves in order to bring up the ark of the LORD, the God of Israel.
>
> ¹⁵And the Levites carried the ark of God with the poles on their shoulders, as Moses had

commanded in accordance with the word of the LORD.

²⁵So David and the elders of Israel and the commanders of units of a thousand went to bring up the ark of the covenant of the LORD from the house of Obed-Edom, with rejoicing. ²⁶Because God had helped the Levites who were carrying the ark of the covenant of the LORD, seven bulls and seven rams were sacrificed.

¹They brought the ark of God and set it inside the tent that David had pitched for it, and they presented burnt offerings and fellowship offerings before God (1 Chron. 15-16:1).

Notice what David identified as the problem: "It was because you, the Levites, did not bring it up the first time that the LORD our God broke out in anger against us. We did not inquire of him about how to do it in the prescribed way" (1 Chron. 15:13). He had the Levites consecrate themselves this time and bear the ark in the prescribed way with the Levites carrying the ark of God with the poles on their shoulders. And thus, the Lord was pleased. You see, neither their good intentions nor their best actions impressed God. Neither the rejoicing nor the songs meant anything to Him. He was looking for obedience, and only obedience satisfied Him.

I can identify three classes of people in the church of God today:

**1.** *Those who hear the word of God and do not do it.* This is typified by Ezekiel's countrymen. I like to call the group Ezekiel's congregation. See what the Lord said about them:

> [30]As for you, son of man, your countrymen are talking together about you by the walls and at the doors of the houses, saying to each other, "Come and hear the message that has come from the LORD."
>
> [31]My people come to you, as they usually do, and sit before you to listen to your words, but they do not put them into practice. With their mouths they express devotion, but their hearts are greedy for unjust gain.
>
> [32]Indeed, to them you are nothing more than one who sings love songs with a beautiful voice and plays an instrument well, for they hear your words but do not put them into practice (Ezek. 33:30-32).

They were not only eager to hear the word of God from Ezekiel, they enjoyed it. In fact, it was as sweet to them as a beautiful love song, but they did not put it into practice. With their mouth they expressed devotion to God but did not do His word. They were like people Jesus described in Matthew 7:21-22 who call Him "Lord, Lord" but do not the will of His Father in heaven. He said such people will not enter the kingdom of heaven. Our churches today are filled with people who delight in coming to church and hearing the word of God and who profess to belong to Christ, but who do not practice the word. The picture I see as I think of this is that of a hen who comes to a sandy place, delves into the sand, and covers herself with it. Then she steps out, shakes off the sand, and simply walks away. Such people come to church and submit themselves to be drenched with the word of God. But as soon as they step out of the church, they shake off the word and walk away the same. Though they claim to be Christians, they don't live it. James describes them as deceivers of themselves. He likens them to a man who looks at himself in a mirror and after looking at himself, goes away and immediately forgets what he looks like (Jas. 1: 22-24).

**2.** *Those who preach the word of God but do not do it.* This describes every professing Christian who does not live the word of God, but much more, it describes those of them who preach the gospel, such as the pastors and evangelists, among others. They are the people Jesus described who will say to Him on that day, "'Lord, Lord, did we not prophesy in your name, and in your name drive out demons and perform many miracles?' Then I will tell them plainly, 'I never knew you. Away from me you evil doers!'" (Matthew 7: 22-23). In spite of what they claim to have done in the name of the Lord, Jesus describes them simply as "evil doers." When you merely profess the word of God and not do it, the Lord simply regards you as an evil doer. That is a food for thought and calls for caution on the part of all who preach the gospel. Paul knew it and that was why he said, "But I discipline my body and bring it into subjection, lest, when I have preached to others, I myself should become disqualified." He knew that God is no respecter of persons and that partial obedience is no obedience to Him. He knew that what will satisfy Him is doing the word also and not preaching it only. Many people think that the mere fact of miracles following their ministry means that they are justified before God. They therefore do not pay attention to their lives. Except when they repent; they will be terribly disappointed on that day. Many others are deceived by signs and wonders following a man's ministry. They think that the miracles manifesting are evidence enough that they are right with God. They follow them and copy everything they do sheepishly without reference to the word of God. Those people too will be disappointed on that day, for God has just one standard. The standard is: "Let every one that nameth the name of Christ depart from iniquity" (2 Tim. 2:19, KJV).

Jesus described the Pharisees and the teachers of the law as hypocrites who do not do what they preach. He said to His disciples and the crowd, "The teachers of the law and the Pharisees sit in Moses' seat. So you must obey them and do everything they tell you. But do not do what they do, for they do not practice what they preach. They tie up heavy loads and put them on men's shoulders, but they themselves are not willing to lift a finger to move them" (Matt. 23:1-3). Note His instruction: "You must obey them and do everything they tell you. But do not do what they do, for they do not practice what they preach." That implies that if you follow what they do, you will be misled.

Because of the first two groups of people, the church is not making the required impact on the world. Such people do not challenge the world. Rather, they are a stumbling block to many who want to come to the Lord. Watching them, the world sees no reason to be like them. If anything, the world regards them as hypocrites who pretend to be what they are not. They misrepresent the Christian faith and Christ Himself. Once, a young man told me concerning his boss who was a believer and indeed a pastor, "If Christianity is like what I see in this man, I will have nothing to do with it." His problem was that the man never practiced what he professed. His life did not agree with his profession.

**3.** *Those who hear, confess, and do the word of God.* Jesus said it is only he who calls Him "Lord, Lord" and does the will of His Father in heaven who will enter the kingdom of heaven (Matt. 7: 21). James says, "²²Do not merely listen to the word, and so deceive yourselves. Do what it says . . . the man who looks intently into the perfect law that gives freedom, and continues to do this, not forgetting what he has heard, but doing it—he will be blessed in what he does" (Jas. 1: 22-25). God is looking for those who will not only hear His word but also do it. He is also looking for those who will not only preach the word but will do it also. In fact, the order is doing first before preaching. Jesus says, "Whoever practices and teaches these commands will be called great in the kingdom of heaven" (Matt. 5:19). The Scripture talks about what Jesus himself began to do and to teach (Acts 1:1). Both doing and preaching the word are important, but I believe that doing is more effective in interpersonal relationship. Preaching, of course, is also important to explain to people why you live the way you do for the avoidance of doubt. Jesus said that when your light shines before men, they will see your good works, not what you say, necessarily, and glorify your father who is in heaven. What shines brighter is what you do, not what you say. What you say, nevertheless, identifies who your Father is so that no one will make the mistake of giving His glory to another. That's why it is important to speak. Ordinary life experience has vindicated the point that action is more effective than words. Hence, people say: *Action speaks louder than words.* The statement acknowledges that words speak loud and stresses the importance of words. But it says that action speaks louder, and that is the point I'm making here. A lifestyle of godly character is more resounding and is a powerful influence on those who are watching. I know what I am saying because I became a believer by watching a life and being attracted by it. Consequently, I desired earnestly to live like him. He was my brother, Henry. I always prayed to God in secret to help me become like him in character. His life kept challenging and convicting me until I repented and surrendered my life to Christ. I think that is why my emphasis in the faith is on "doing" more than "talking." To me, profession of faith that is not coupled with doing the word is nothing at all. The Christianity I saw that attracted me was the one that was depicted to me much more by action. Of course, Henry shared the word with me occasionally, but what won me was how he lived—a lifestyle that was beyond ordinary. The Bible talks about believing wives winning their unbelieving husbands without a word by their good conduct (1 Pet. 3:1). I think the problem of Christianity today is that there is too much emphasis on speaking and too little emphasis on doing, and that is why the church is not challenging the world. When you merely preach the word and live a contradictory lifestyle, your lifestyle wipes away the effect of your word. At best, you produce hypocrites like you, and that is the bane of the Christianity of our time. Jesus said to the Pharisees and teachers of the law who did the same, "Woe to you, teachers of the law and Pharisees, you hypocrites! You travel over land and sea to win a single convert, and when he becomes one, you make him twice as much a son of hell as you are" (Matt. 23:15). What did Jesus promise them? Woe and hell.

> **God is looking for those who will not only hear His word but also do it. He is also looking for those who will not only preach the word but will do it also.**

Hear Jesus's illustration of the matter in Matthew 6: 46-49:

> 46Why do you call me, "Lord, Lord," and do not do what I say?
>
> 47I will show you what he is like who comes to me and hears my words and puts them into practice.

---

**A lifestyle of godly character is more resounding and is a powerful influence on those who are watching.**

---

> 48He is like a man building a house, who dug down deep and laid the foundation on rock. When a flood came, the torrent struck that house but could not shake it, because it was well built.
>
> 49But the one who hears my words and does not put them into practice is like a man who built a house on the ground without a foundation. The moment the torrent struck that house, it collapsed and its destruction was complete.

You will be tested for what you are, and the test will reveal it. Those who are genuine will stand the test, but those who are not will collapse and be exposed.

James describes faith without works as dead and useless. Hear him:

> 14What good is it, my brothers, if a man claims to have faith but has no deeds? Can such faith save him?
>
> 15Suppose a brother or sister is without clothes and daily food.

[16]If one of you says to him, "Go, I wish you well; keep warm and well fed," but does nothing about his physical needs, what good is it? [17]In the same way, faith by itself, if it is not accompanied by action, is dead.

[18]But someone will say, "You have faith; I have deeds."

Show me your faith without deeds, and I will show you my faith by what I do.

[19]You believe that there is one God. Good! Even the demons believe that—and shudder.

[20]You foolish man, do you want evidence that faith without deeds is useless?

[21]Was not our ancestor Abraham considered righteous for what he did when he offered his son Isaac on the altar?

[22]You see that his faith and his actions were working together, and his faith was made complete by what he did.

[23]And the scripture was fulfilled that says, "Abraham believed God, and it was credited to him as righteousness," and he was called God's friend.

[24]You see that a person is justified by what he does and not by faith alone.

[25]In the same way, was not even Rahab the prostitute considered righteous for what she did when she gave lodging to the spies and sent them off in a different direction?

[26]As the body without the spirit is dead, so faith without deeds is dead (Jas. 2:14-26).

God expects us to match our profession of faith with action. Our profession of faith is incomplete if it is not accompanied by action. That is how to shine for Him in total obedience. When we are obedient this way, we do two things: 1.) We show God that we love Him; 2.) We show men that we love God. And God is glorified. May we arise and shine for the glory of God.

# Chapter Ten

## No Reason for Strife

We live in a world full of strife. Strife is rife among kingdoms, nations, communities, groups, organizations, churches, families, and individuals, among others. It is behind the wars and unhealthy competitions and rivalry that are found everywhere. It comes with greed, jealousy, envy, deceit, hatred, killing, maiming, and all kinds of vices. The Scripture aptly says, "For where you have envy and selfish ambition, there you find disorder and every evil practice" (Jas. 3: 16). That describes our world today. Strife dates back to the beginning of the world. It was behind the rivalry between Cain and Abel, Esau and Jacob, as well as Joseph and his brothers. It was also behind the opposition of Moses and Aaron by Korah, Dathan and Abiram. As well, it was behind the opposition of Moses by Miriam and Aaron. It was behind the request made by the sons of Zebedee, James and John, that both occupy the left and right sides of Jesus respectively, in His kingdom. And it was behind the killing of Jesus by the Pharisees and Scribes. It is a product of envy, jealousy, greed, and selfish ambition.

We want to see the mind of God on the subject matter of strife for His children as it is an ill wind in the church. The result of strife in the church is division, uncoordinated battle against the kingdom of darkness, and unnecessary duplication of efforts. What we see is, as in the Corinthian church, "I follow Paul," "I follow Apollos," "I follow Cephas," and "I follow Jesus." (1 Corinthians 1: 12). It is important to address this matter, as it concerns the church of God because the Scripture says, "Every kingdom divided against itself will be ruined, and every city or household divided against itself will not stand" (Matt. 12:25). To see the mind of God, let us look at the body network as presented in 1 Corinthians 12:12-30:

> **The result of strife in the church is division, uncoordinated battle against the kingdom of darkness, and unnecessary duplication of efforts.**

¹²The body is a unit, though it is made up of many parts; and though all its parts are many, they form one body. So it is with Christ.

¹³For we were all baptized by one Spirit into one body—whether Jews or Greeks, slave or free—and we were all given the one Spirit to drink.

¹⁴Now the body is not made up of one part but of many.

¹⁵If the foot should say, "Because I am not a hand, I do not belong to the body," it would not for that reason cease to be part of the body.

¹⁶And if the ear should say, "Because I am not an eye, I do not belong to the body," it would not for that reason cease to be part of the body.

¹⁷If the whole body were an eye, where would the sense of hearing be? If the whole body were an ear, where would the sense of smell be?

¹⁸But in fact God has arranged the parts in the body, every one of them, just as he wanted them to be.

¹⁹If they were all one part, where would the body be?

²⁰As it is, there are many parts, but one body.

²¹The eye cannot say to the hand, "I don't need you!" And the head cannot say to the feet, "I don't need you!"

²²On the contrary, those parts of the body that seem to be weaker are indispensable,

²³and the parts that we think are less honorable we treat with special honor. And the parts that are unpresentable are treated with special modesty,

²⁴while our presentable parts need no special treatment. But God has combined the members of the body and has given greater honor to the parts that lacked it,

²⁵so that there should be no division in the body, but that its parts should have equal concern for each other.

²⁶If one part suffers, every part suffers with it; if one part is honored, every part rejoices with it.

²⁷Now you are the body of Christ, and each one of you is a part of it.

²⁸And in the church God has appointed first of all apostles, second prophets, third teachers, then workers of miracles, also those having gifts of healing, those able to help others, those with

gifts of administration, and those speaking in different kinds of tongues.

²⁹Are all apostles? Are all prophets? Are all teachers? Do all work miracles?

³⁰Do all have gifts of healing? Do all speak in tongues? Do all interpret?

In the above account, the purpose of God for the church is revealed. The body, though a unit, has many parts, and each part has its different function for the good of the body. The purpose of God is that there should be mutual appreciation among the members of the church and that there should be unity in diversity. In combining the parts of the body the way He has done, God's wisdom is that there should be no division in the body, and that its parts should have equal concern for each other (v. 25). In this, God means to explain to the church His purpose in appointing people into different offices and to teach her how to function as a body. In the body system, there is no strife, no competition, and no rivalry among the parts. Instead, there is harmony. This is how God expects His church to function.

> **The purpose of God is that there should be mutual appreciation among the members of the church and that there should be unity in diversity.**

Let us see another illustration of God's mind and expectation:

¹⁴Again, it will be like a man going on a journey, who called his servants and entrusted his property to them.

¹⁵To one he gave five talents of money, to another two talents, and to another one talent, each according to his ability. Then he went on his journey.

¹⁶The man who had received the five talents went at once and put his money to work and gained five more.

¹⁷So also, the one with the two talents gained two more.

¹⁸But the man who had received the one talent went off, dug a hole in the ground and hid his master's money.

¹⁹After a long time the master of those servants returned and settled accounts with them.

²⁰The man who had received the five talents brought the other five. "Master," he said, "you entrusted me with five talents. See, I have gained five more."

²¹His master replied, "Well done, good and faithful servant! You have been faithful with a few things; I will put you in charge of many things. Come and share your master's happiness!"

²²The man with the two talents also came. "Master," he said, "you entrusted me with two talents; see, I have gained two more."

²³His master replied, "Well done, good and faithful servant! You have been faithful with a few things; I will put you in charge of many things. Come and share your master's happiness!"

²⁴Then the man who had received the one talent came. "Master," he said, "I knew that you are a hard man, harvesting where you have not

sown and gathering where you have not scattered seed.

²⁵So I was afraid and went out and hid your talent in the ground. See, here is what belongs to you."

²⁶His master replied, "You wicked, lazy servant! So you knew that I harvest where I have not sown and gather where I have not scattered seed?

²⁷Well then, you should have put my money on deposit with the bankers, so that when I returned I would have received it back with interest.

²⁸Take the talent from him and give it to the one who has the ten talents (Matt. 25:14-28).'

God has made each of us different and given us different gifts and talents according to our respective abilities. He will demand account of us based on what He has given us and our abilities, not based on what we did not receive. You are required to use your gift and talent according to your ability. To whom much is given, from him much is required; and to whom much has been committed, of him much will be demanded (Lk. 12: 48). The only way to gain an increase in what you have is by being faithful with what you received. When you do this, you will gain increase in two definite ways:

1. *Multiplication.* When you put your talent to use, you gain an increase through multiplication. If it is money, you gain more money; if it is talent, your skill is sharpened, which translates to higher productivity and higher returns. Practice, they say, makes perfect. Athletes understand this point very well. There are some more gifted athletes who do not put their talents to use. With time, they become blunt and lose their ability due to lack of use. On the other hand, there are some

less gifted ones who put theirs to use. With constant practice, they become better and turn great and famous athletes.

2. *Reward of faithfulness.* When the account is taken, you will receive a raise if you are faithful. The master said to each of the two faithful servants, "Well done, good and faithful servant! You have been faithful with a few things; I will put you in charge of many things" (vs. 21 and 23). They gained more as a reward of faithfulness. This is the practice in workplaces. Each worker is assigned a role. At set times, an appraisal is done, and those who have been dutiful and productive are rewarded either by way of promotion or pay raise.

God has assigned roles to each member of the church, and all He expects is faithfulness (1 Cor. 4:2), not strife. Notice that the servant who grumbled lost everything in the end. God expects us to focus on our role and play it well. We are not required to grumble and compare ourselves with others foolishly. John the Baptist was one man who exemplified this point wonderfully. One day, Jesus and His disciples went to Judean countryside, and Jesus spent some time with them and baptized. John also was baptizing at Aenon near Salim. An argument developed between some of John's disciples and a certain Jew over the issue of ceremonial washing. "They came to John and said to him, 'Rabbi, that man who was with you on the other side of the Jordan—the one you testified about—well, he is baptizing, and everyone is going to him'" (Jn. 3:26). That statement, "everyone is going to him," was very provoking. It was good enough to arouse envy and jealousy in John. Before now, John was the one person who was baptizing and to whom everyone went. Hence, he was called John the Baptist. His identity was baptism. And behold, another man, Jesus, arose also baptizing, and the report was brought to John informing him that the man "is baptizing, and everyone is going to him." That was a big test for John. The implication of the statement was that this man is stealing the show from John. They wanted to know what John had to say about it. To this John, amazingly, replied:

> A man can receive only what is given him from heaven.
>
> [28]You yourselves can testify that I said, "I am not the Christ but am sent ahead of him."
>
> [29]The bride belongs to the bridegroom. The friend who attends the bridegroom waits and listens for him, and is full of joy when he hears the bridegroom's voice. That joy is mine, and it is now complete.
>
> [30]He must become greater; I must become less.
>
> [31]The one who comes from above is above all; the one who is from the earth belongs to the earth, and speaks as one from the earth. The one who comes from heaven is above all.
>
> [32]He testifies to what he has seen and heard, but no one accepts his testimony.
>
> [33]The man who has accepted it has certified that God is truthful.
>
> [34]For the one whom God has sent speaks the words of God, for God gives the Spirit without limit.
>
> [35]The Father loves the Son and has placed everything in his hands.
>
> [36]Whoever believes in the Son has eternal life, but whoever rejects the Son will not see life, for God's wrath remains on him (John 3: 27- 36).

John's answer revealed a deep truth about life we all need to know and assimilate. The truth is: "A man can receive only what is given him from heaven." Whatever a man has is not his making. It is given him from heaven by God. Simple. No arguments. You don't need to fight over it. If you need it, look up—ask heaven. You can only receive yours from there. John then called their attention to the fact that he never pretended to be the Christ. He was only sent ahead of Him to prepare the way for Him. He declared the full extent of his joy following the development. To him, what was happening was fulfilling his testimony about Christ, and that gave him great joy. John understood his role and played it satisfactorily—he was Jesus's forerunner. He also understood Jesus's role and announced it ahead of time. He was now happy that Jesus had appeared on stage to play it. We are all like actors on stage with different roles. Every actor is required to play his role in order to complete the drama. Some people have more prominent roles to play than others, but each role is important. That is how life is. John spent time extolling Jesus. He made this awe-inspiring statement: "He must become greater; I must become less" (v. 30). KJV puts it thus: "He must increase, but I must decrease." That should be our goal and attitude in life—to have Him increase while we decrease. John's answer also shows contentment. John was such a humble man. No wonder he was highly esteemed by Jesus. Jesus said of him, "Verily I say unto you, Among them that are born of women there hath not risen a greater than John the Baptist" (Matt. 11:11, KJV). He operated in a supernatural realm. A man operating in the natural realm would have started striving with Jesus given the fame he was already enjoying. But John was content with what God gave him.

The apostle Peter once found himself in a position where he began to look sideways—comparing himself with another. One day, as Jesus spoke with Peter, indicating the kind of death by which he (Peter) would glorify God, Peter turned and saw John. Then he asked Jesus, "Lord, what about him?" (Jn.

21:21), referring to John. Jesus answered him, saying, "If I will that he remain till I come, what is that to you? You follow Me." (v. 22). Jesus saw the heart of Peter in asking that question. Peter wanted to engage in unnecessary comparison, and Jesus decided to hush him and teach him how to think. He taught him not to pry into the affairs of others but to focus on his walk with God: "If I will that he remain till I come, what is that to you? [what is your business?]. You follow Me [As for you, follow Me]." That is the message. We should not pry into the lives of others. Paul put it straight when he said to the Thessalonian church, "Make it your ambition to lead a quiet life, to mind your own business . . ." (I Thess. 4: 11). The point is: mind your own business—no meddling, no poking or sniffing around, and no tale-bearing.

Are we then saying that you should not care about what happens to your brother? Not at all. We are saying, rather, that you should not be envious or jealous of your brother; neither should you begrudge him his success nor make unnecessary comparisons with him. Of course, God wants us to identify with one another positively. He wants us to be one another's keeper and bear one another's burden (Gal. 6:2). He wants us to rejoice with them that rejoice and mourn with them that mourn (Rom. 12:15), just like the parts of the body. For when one part suffers, every part suffers with it, and when one part is honored, every part rejoices with it (1 Cor. 12: 26). God also wants us to spur one another unto love and good works (Heb. 10:12). He wants us to draw inspiration and encouragement from one another as iron sharpens iron (Prov. 27:17). Recently, I reconnected with an old Christian friend after many years. As we flashed back and shared about our days in the Young People's Fellowship of our church to which we belonged, he shared with me a testimony about himself that I never knew about. He told me that when he joined the fellowship, he was challenged by the way youths like him understood and shared the Scriptures. He said he went home and cried unto God to help him study and understand the Bible like those young people. For days, he locked himself in his room, fasted, and prayed and studied the Scriptures. Provoked by his fellow youths' walk with God, he earnestly sought God and found Him. The young man soon became one of the most respected brothers in the fellowship and in the church because of his obvious deep relationship with God. He manifested deep understanding of the Scriptures as well as spiritual gifts. That is the kind of thing God expects. Even now, remembering some of my Christian friends in Nigeria spurs me on in the Lord. Remembering their fervency in spirit makes me fervent in spirit; remembering their faithfulness makes me strive unto faithfulness. I see them as fellow soldiers of the Lord, and I get strengthened remembering they are there. We inspire and challenge one another. That is how iron sharpens iron.

God has called us unto love for one another and not unto envy and strife. Jesus says our identity should be love and that by showing it one to another, all men shall know that we are His disciples (Jn. 13: 35). He left us an example that we may follow in His steps in this matter. The Scripture says:

> ⁵Your attitude should be the same as that of Christ Jesus:
>
> ⁶Who, being in very nature God, did not consider equality with God something to be grasped, ⁷but made himself nothing, taking the very nature of a servant, being made in human likeness.
>
> ⁸And being found in appearance as a man, he humbled himself and became obedient to death—even death on a cross! (Phillip. 2:5-8).

The point to note here is that Jesus did not consider God His rival. As His disciples, we should not consider our brethren our rivals but as partners and co-laborers in God's vineyard. When this is our perception, then we can work together and overcome the kingdom of darkness. Also, God expects us to be content with what we have. As the Scripture puts it, "godliness with contentment is great gain. For we brought nothing into the world, and we can take nothing out of it. But if we have food and clothing, we will be content with that" (1 Tim. 6:6-8). For it is God who works in us both to will and to do of His good pleasure (Phillip. 2: 13).

# Decision Guide

If you want to accept Jesus into your life, pray with all your heart, confess your sins to God for forgiveness, and invite Jesus into your heart as your Lord and Savior. He will forgive you and come into your heart. Follow this up by joining a Bible-believing church where you will be taught and nurtured with the sincere milk of the Word of God so you can grow thereby (1 Peter 2:2). God bless you in Jesus's name. Amen.

# References

TanBible.com, "200 Amazing Hymn Stories," prepared by staff, Bible Communications, Inc. http://www.tanbible.com/tol_sng/itiswellwithmysoul. htm.

Oremus.org, "My God, how wonderful thou art," from *Ancient & Modern*, Standard Edition, 1875-1924 by F. Faber http://www.oremus. org/hymnal/amstd.html.

Harrison, E.M. 1954. "David Livingstone: The Pathfinder of Africa" from *Giants of the Missionary Trail.* http://www.wholesomewords.org/missions/giants/biol ivingstone.html.

Jeremiah, D. *Living with Confidence in a Chaotic World: What on Earth Should We Do Now?* Nashville, TN: Thomas Nelson, 2009.

Johnston, J. H. *Fifty Missionary Heroes.* Salem, OH: Schmul Publishing Co., 2001.

*The Voice of Martyrs Blog;* "Pelagius-AD 925," blog entry by Karen, October 4, 2010.

Uma, U. 2006. "Day God refused to hear my prayer," *Eternal life Christian Online magazine.* Accessed July 2, 2010, http://www.elifeonline.net/elife4-jan-2006/interview-uma-ukpai (site discontinued).

WorldNetDaily, "Teen's testimony of faith unstopped by death," posted by Anonymous, October 26, 2006, accessed February 12, 2011, http://www.wnd.com/?pageId=38540.

Wurmbrand, R. *Tortured for Christ.* Bartlesville, OK: Living Sacrifice Book Company, 1998.